GURU GRANTH SAHIB OVER TO THE WEST

Idea of Sikh Scriptures Translations : 1810-1909

Nazer Singh

Commonwealth

Guru Granth Sahib Over to the West

Ist Edition : 2005
ISBN 81-311-0019-7

Published by :
Ajay Verma
For Commonwealth Publishers
4831/24, Prahlad Street,
Ansari Road, Darya Ganj,
New Delhi - 110002
Phone : 23272541, 23257835
Fax: 91-011-23257835
E-mail : campusbooks@hotmail.com

Laser Typesetting by :
Stylish Laser Typesetter
Delhi

Printed at :
Roshan Offset Printers
Delhi

Preface

This small book of articles deals with the British discovery of Sikhs, their literature and history. Enquiry was diplomatic and military during the 18th century. However, the Anglo-Sikh relations after the fall of Delhi and Hansi into the hands of Company in 1803 and more so the Sikh Treaties of January 1806 and April 1809 with the British widened the scope of the enquiry. With Malcolm's work published in 1810, the Punjabi and Sikh writings especially the bani of the Gurus or its elaborations by the Bhai's such as Gurdass and Mani Singh entered the field under investigation. Sikh History and Religion emerged as a common genre by the middle of the 19th century. J.D. Cunningham gave a firm basis to this genre, though H.H. Wilson had acted differently in 1848.

The use of Bani, Sakhi and Rahit by the British, the Christian Missions, the early Nirankaris and the Namdharis necessitated the further opening of Sikh Scriptures. By 1857 the idea of having translation of them was conceived. First attempt in this regard took twenty years *i.e.* 1857-1877. The attempt was official and made through Trumpp. These twenty years also saw the printing of the Adi Granth in the Damdama Bir twice *i.e.* in 1864 and 1868 in Lahore. A Janam-Sakhi (Bhai Bala version) was also printed.

Trumpp's translation project (1869-75) raised the issue of the concept of Scripture in Sikh tradition. The issues debated were the status and role of the Dassam Granth, and the significance of the Rahitnamas. But at a more fundamental level, the issues were : (1) the role of Guru Gobind Singh and the political ideas and practice of Khalsa, and (2) the precise relationship between Sikhism and Hinduism. The missions and the early Nirankaris preferred Guru Nanak and the Adi Granth while the followers of Baba Ram Singh had a marked preference for the code of Khalsa based upon the Granth Sahib including the Rahitnamas and the Dassam Granth. By the end of 1871, the British administration dropped the idea of having the Dassam Granth translated by Trumpp. By 1873 the idea was dropped altogether. Trumpp translated the Adi Granth but not in totality. He had a sound understanding of the Janam Sakhi tradition. But it was not so in the case of Sikh Scripture.

The Rahitnama literature and the Adi Granth became politically significant with the rise of the Kukas or Guru Ram Singh's 'Sant Khalsa'. The Namdharis of Bhaini questioned the Sikh Rahit current in the historic Gurudwaras. The Mahants protected by a section of the Nihungs disapproved the Kuka 'innovations' in the Rahit. The traditional Rahit had already been patronized by the British Military authorities. The Namdharis fought a lost battle. By 1877, the Adi Granth had entered the British educational system in the Punjab.

Trumpp's failure to satisfy both the administration and the Sikhs led indirectly to the revival of Sikh Historiography of the Cunningham kind. It was a Historiography that stood for (1) the unity of Religion and History, (II) the oneness of ten Sikh Gurus, (III) organic link between the philosophy of Guru Gobind Singh and the political actions of the Khalsa, (IV) need to reconcile the Khalsa and the British, and (V) the uniqueness of Sikh world view. M.A. Macauliffe was the architect of this revival, though his path had been cleared by 'the historical' works of L. Griffin and 'the educational work' of G.W. Leitner. All the three endeavoured to make the British as the trustees of Sikh heritage.

One of these articles—comprising our chapter two here—has been published in *Journal of Sikh Studies* (Vol. XIX, 1995 (pp. 35-46). Except this one, the others are being presented for the first time. Even then, the author's papers in *Proceedings of the Punjab History Conference for the year 1999*, and *Journal of Sikh Studies* (Vol. XXIII, 1999) may be a further useful reading in this context.

A number of individuals have helped me in making this collection. The author is thankful to all such friends.

Nazer Singh

Contents

1 The Sikh Scriptures and History

What are the most important Sikh ideals and institutions today? Reverence for Gurbani in the Adi Granth and History-writing aught to be the answer. History be there because it had become a part of sikh worship. Ardas, the prayer, enjoins to fix thought on the Holy Granth. It also reminds the deeds of Khalsa.[1] Gurbani and History are meditated upon as if Gurbani worked through the Khalsa.

Sabad and Sakhi had been the original institutions of the Panth since its very inception. Janam Sakhi or the early Sikh historiography enabled the Sikhs to emerge as a distinct socio-religious community ordained by the Divine.[2] The British Sikh Studies as well as the Sikh reformations during the 19th century invested the Adi Granth with a significance that was higher than that in the Janam Sakhi tradition. Sikhism began

1. M.A. Macauliffe thought it proper to close his work on 'the Lives and writtings of the ten Guru's with Ardas that he had translated to provide a 'suitable end' to his presentation. Recently, Surjit Hans had used the Sikh prayer to show the theological and sociological characteristics of a Sikh, See, M.A. Macauliffe, *The Sikh Religion,* Vol.V (rpt) (Satvic Books, 2000) pp. 331-32, and Surjit Hans, 'The Secular Heritage of the Sikhs', in *Sikh History and Religion in the Twentieth Century* edited by Joseph T.O' Connel and others (Manohar, 1990), p. 71.
2. W.H. McLeod has treated this subject exhaustively in his work *Early Sikh Tradition : A Study of the Janam-Sakhi* (Clarendon Press, Oxford, 1980) Surjit Hans has commented upon McLeod's book to highlight the significance of the work, See, his article 'Early Sikh Tradition', in *Journal of Regional History,* Vol. I, 1980, pp. 175-88.

to be defined through Gurbani.[3] The early Nirankaris and the Namdharis attempted it. E.Trumpp failed to grasp this development. M.A. Macauliffe actually did it. Bhai Kahn Singh Nabha took the Adi Granth as a 'witness' to his Ham Hindu Nahin character.[4] Gurbani and History fashioned the Singh identity.

The Adi Granth emerged as the sole Sikh Scripture in the first instance. Secondly, its socialization through the Namdhari, the Singh Sabha and the Nirankari movements as well as by the print industry made it the most acknowledged scripture. Today, it is for the Sikhs "their exclusive scripture."[5]

Who did know the spiritual and material value of literature and translation more than the House of Guru Teg Bahadur? The Gurdarbar was established by the ninth Guru.[6] His Hukamnamas show the excellence of his office both in the Punjab and in the east.[7] It could, and in fact, did, work in the absence of the Guru also. The Sangat of Patna stood instructed as to how it should care for the leasure of child Govind. It was done through a Hukamnamma. In turn, the Bachittar Natak spoke of the piety of tenth Guru's father and mother. Hero of the Natak remembered the nurses who brought him up at Paunta.[8] In fact, 'Apni Katha', the thirty three Swayias and

3. Gurbani as a source of Sikhism and its History began to occupay an important place in the western presentations of the Sikh movement during the 19th century. For an out line of this development one can start with *Sketch of the Sikhs* by John Malcolm.

4. For a more recent view of Kahn Singh Nabha and his work 'Ham Hindu Nahin Hain, See, J.S. Grewal, *Historical Perspectives on Sikh Identity*, Patiala, 1997, pp. 81-100.

5. *Ibid.*, pp. 88, 97.

6. The biographers of Guru Gobind Singh had noticed the relevance of darbar of Guru Teg Bahadur for the education and culture of the 10th Guru, See, J.S. Grewal and S.S. Bal, *Guru Gobind Singh* (Chandigarh, 1987), pp. 38-39.

7. See, S.S. Sagar, *Hukamnamas of Guru Tegh Bahadur* (Amritsar, 2002), p. 41.

8. M.A. Macauliff's translation of the Bachitar Natak reads 'I was born in Patna City, And *afterwards* taken to the Punjab, where nurses of different kinds fondled me, And tended my body in every way', See, Macauliffe, *op. cit.*, p. 303.

Zafarnama came to make the foundation of 18th century Sikh historiography.[9] In short, the Gurdarbar practice of Gurbani and translation confered upon History an equally high honour. The Sikh historiography survived Guru Gobind Singh and his Khalsa.

How was it that 19th century foe of Khalsa, the British, found the traditional Sikh historical method useful for themselves?[10] The answer cannot be essay. One explanation may be offered. The colonial military and diplomatic observers of the Sikhs saw Guru Gobind Singh as the author of their political system having two salients. One, an intense patriotism. Second, love for human and religious equality. Both these featurers were indigenous, they thought. For this very reason Sikh polity was anti-muslim and anti caste, they believed.

But colonial observers were quick to notice that the egalitarian and patriotic teachings of the Gurus were no longer a living principle with the Sardars of Khalsa as it was evidant from the state of Sikh commonwealth that stood marked by mutual jealousies and conflict.[11] The Sikh chiefs and the priests were unable to inspire the comon man. The colonial power stepped into to accomplish the task unfulfilled. It was done in the name of Punjab and its defence against the Afghans.[12] It was achieved through the political instrumentality of 'protection' to the Sardars of Malwa and Sarhind and the 'friendship' with the chiefs of Kapurthala and Lahore.

At the ideological level, instrument used was the discovery

9. In a way in a work like Gursobha, one can hear the echos of Bachitar Natak, the Swayias and Zafarnama. For hints of this development, See, Surjit Hans, *A Reconstruction of Sikh History from Sikh Literature* (Jallundhar, 1988), chpts. 8-9.

10. Both John Malcolm and J.D. Cunningham consciously gave due importance to 'Sikh' and 'Punjabi' authors while writting on the Sikhs. See, Nazer Singh, *Delhi and Punjab Essays in History and Historiography* (New Delhi, 1995), chp. I.

11. Malcolm underlined this fact towards the end of his first part in *Sketch of the Sikhs,* dealing with the political history of the Sikhs.

12. Nazer Singh, *op. cit.,* pp. 3, 5.

of Sikh literature—the historical works. Histories were prepared and wrote to promote peace and reconciliation between the Sikhs and the Company. Materially, the British military system came as an alternate opening for the Singhs. Their ways were to be known and they were to be administered the British ways. In this communication or exchange the key was History to be followed by Education.[13]

Yet it would be both ideal and *ahistorical* to think that the British rule accompanied by the Missions and the Sikh reform movements did not influence or alter Sikh Historiography. For one thing some of the European writers showed a marked preference for the Nanak Panth and the Adi Granth over the Khalsa and its literary tradition. Malcolm's concern with Guru Nanak was both political and ideological one.[14] H.H. Wilson had little appreciation for Guru Gobind Singh and his ideas. Wilson disapproved the doctorine of the book and the sword.[15] In 1859, R.N. Cust proclaimed Guru Nanak as an Indian reformer.[16] A Missionary Conference held at Lahore in Dec. 1862 deliberated over the relevance of Sikh literature and tradition to the future of Christianity in the region.[17] "As the influence of Nanak's teaching was for good, so was that of Govind for evil", the conference was told in writting. And the worst evil attributed to the founder of Khalsa was that he 'abused the principles of Nanak to lay the foundations of Sikh

13. *Ibid.,* pp. 51-74.

14. See, Nazer Singh, 'History of Sikh Scriptures' Translations : Idea upto Trumpp', *Journal of Sikh Studies,* Vol. XIX, 1995, p. 40.

15. For a handy reference to H.H.Wilson's treatment of Sikhism in 1848, See, J.S. Grewal, *Contesting Interpretations of the Sikh Tradition* (Manohar, 1998), pp. 27-29.

16. Written in 1859, R.N. Cust's article can be seen in Guru Nanak's birth Quincentenary volume of the *Punjab Past and Present,* Vol. III, 1969, pp. 158-68.

17. See, Rev. William Keene's essay 'The Sikhs : All that can be said about them, From a Missionary Point of View' in the printed Report of the Ninth Session of the Missionary Conference held at Lahore on 31 Dec. - 1st January 1863. The Report was published by the Ludhiana Mission Press. The date of publication is not mentioned, pp. 261-68.

Independence'. In the process, the Guru roused 'the very worst passions of the soul' that made, in turn, the Sikhs as a people without morality, it was added.

This western tendency to divide the Sikh movement and its past into 'good' and 'evil' components represented by Guru Nanak and Guru Gobind Singh, respectively, was so strong that any contrary treatment was difficult to make.

The ill treatment given to J.D. Cunningham's work is a common fact of the Sikh Studies under the British. But it would be useful to recall that Cunningham's 'single movement'[18] thesis stood for the unity of the ten Gurus and for the continuation of Sikh life down to the Anglo-Sikh Wars. He was impressed by the pure patriotism and high hopes of 'the youthful Khalsa'. Cunningham's removal from the political service was the termination of the Sikh historical method centred on the principle of the Divinity and unity of the Gurus leading to the Khalsa practice of grounding their polity in the tenets of Sikhism and the custom of the country.

The missionary records on the Nirankaris and the British reports on the Namdhari movemens show the prominence of the Sikh Scriptures in the teachings of the founders of these movements.[19] A Ludhiana mission report of 1853 says that the Nirankaris had been active for the last eight or nine years, though they could't and did't work in the open as 'fear kept

18. J.D. Cunningham's method have been approved by a number of Sikh scholars such as Teja Singh, Ganda Singh, J.S. Grewal and S.S. Bal. *A Short History of the Sikhs* by Teja Singh and Ganda Singh, and S.S. Bal's article on Cunningham's attempt to rehabitate himself into the British Political Service published in Harbans Singh and N.G. Barrier, *Essays in Honour of Dr. Ganda Singh* (Patiala : 1976), pp. 215-33. Also See, J.S. Grewal, *Contesting Interpretations, op. cit.*, pp. 29-33.

19. For the Nirankaris, See, Harbans Singh, *The Heritage of the Sikhs.* This book was first published in 1964 from London. Its revised reprint was issued by the Manohar in 1983. We have used second edition published by the Manohar in 1994.

The Namdharis have been dealt with in *Kukian de Vithia* by Ganda Singh, and in, *Kuka Movement* by Fauja Singh.

them quiet'.[20] But the extension of the Company's Government made them more bold. Further, the Nirankaris "with the assistance of our religious publications to furnish them with arguments against idolatry ... attacked the faith of the Hindus more fiercely'.[21] The report further reads :[22]

> They professedly reject idolatery, and all reverence and respect for whatever is held sacred by Sikhs or Hindus, except Nanak and his Granth.

They were called Nirankaris, says the report, "from their belief in God, as a spirit without bodily form". The second principle of their faith was that salvation could be achieved through the meditation on God, and they regard Nanak as their savior' as he had taught them the way of salvation. The report clearly says that their morning worship was congregational and it consisted of bowing the head to the ground before the Granth, making offerings, and in hearing the (Holy) book read by one of them or explained by their leader if present.

The Namdharis attracted the British administration's attention in March, 1863.[23] The Police Memorandum of June 1863 quoted a letter received by Mahant Narain Singh of Amritsar. The police said it was the letter passing the following instructions of 'the Kooka Guru' to his followers :[24]

> Sing the Granth together, and the praise of the Deity; be affraid of none, abuse no one ... whoever makes money by the marriage of his daughter is a rascal (badmash), whoever commits infanticide or exchange his daughter is equally so. Your children should be educated in the precepts of the Granth.

---

20. The Ludhiana Mission Report, 1853, Quoted in Harban Singh, *op. cit.*, p. 191.
21. *Ibid.*
22. *Ibid.*
23. Ganda Singh, *Kukian de Vithia,* (Patiala, 2000), p. 15.
24. *Ibid.*, p. 15.

Commenting upon the letter, the Memorandum says about the Kukas, "The Granth is their only inspired volume".[25]

Similarly an another officer in the same Memorandum reported that in the Namdhari article of faith 'Gobind Singh's Granth' was "the only true one, written by inspiration, and is the only sacred writing existent. Gobind Singh is the only Guru."[26] The officer was Kinchant.

Interestingly, the modern scholars of Sikhism and Sikh history had positively relied upon these mission and police sources to present the Nirankari and Namdhari Movements. For example, Harbans Singh in *The Heritage of the Sikhs,* interpreted the above mentioned mission report of 1853 as to give the following meaning to the early Nirankari movement :[27]

> In its emphasis on the primacy of the Guru Granth in the Sikh system and on self-identity, the Nirankari movement foreshadowed the principal concerns of the Singh Sabha reformation.

Harbans Singh does not stop at that. He treats the mission report of 1853 as theoretically significant for it "falsifies the hastily advanced view that the new sense of self consciousness among the Sikhs was the creation of British Policy".[28]

Likewise, Ganda Singh as well as Fauja Singh[29] quotes Kinchant to show how important was the Sikh Scripture for the Kuka reformation. They surely takes Kinchant's reference to 'Gobind Singh's Granth' as the one made to the Holy Granth. Further, Fauja Singh rejects Ganda Singh's view that the Sau-Sakhi was the ideological basis of 'Guru Ram Singh's entire power'. For him, it was not the Sakhi book "but the Holy Granth which was to serve as the guide of the neophyts".[30]

---

25. *Ibid.*
26. *Ibid.*
27. Harbans Singh, *op. cit.,* p. 191.
28. *Ibid.*
29. *Kuka Movement,* Motilal and Banarsidass, 1965, pp. 22-23.
30. *Ibid.,* p. 23.

Going by the modern Sikh historians of the Namdharies, Baba Ram Singh recognized the Damdamma bir as the Guru Granth and emphatically told his followers to follow its teachings. What was his attitude towards the Dassam Granth? A recent study of the movement suggest that the Kuka leader "in acknowledging the 'great code' came to view the Adi Granth and the Dassam Granth' as being at par."[31] Given Baba Ram Singh's concern with Guru Gobind Singh and the Khalsa tradition, it might be so. After all, he had denominated his followers as 'the Sant Khalsa' in 1857.

Be as it may, Baba Ram Singh used the Sikh Scripturers to question the legitimacy of Sikh and Hindu clergy to hold the places of worship to preach a religion that was, in fact, the Gurudom of the Sodhis, Bedis, Mahants and Brahmins. His own creed was open to all 'irrespective of caste and religion'. It regarded the Mandirs and Shivdwaras as the means of extortion and the idols and the idol-worship as 'insulting to God'. By 1867, he had openly confronted the Sikh priests to whom he had found acting contrary to the precepts of the Guru Granth by their various acts including infanticide.[32] The priests, interestingly protected by the Nihungs, charged Ram Singh that he had violated the Khalsa code by making a different and new Rahit. Obviously, these arguments and counter-arguments had raised the issue of the authenticity of Sikh tradition and literature including the scriptures.

The year 1857 was not only the year of birth of Baba Ram Singh's Sant Khalsa but was also the one that saw a change in the British attitude towards the Sikh ruling sections as well as the Sikh material tradition. On the advice of Nihal Singh Chhachhi, a Sardar from Rawalpindi area, it was decided to enlist the Sikhs in the British Indian army. What kind of Sikhs

31. Jaswinder Singh, Kuka Movement (New Delhi, 1985), p.15 quoted in Harjot Oberoi, *The Construction of Religious Boundaries* (Delhi, 1997), p. 200.

32. This list of the acts of violation of the Rahit committed by the Pujaris and the others included, the meat-eating, drinking of wine, speaking untruth, adultery and infanticide, See, Ganda Singh, *Vithia, op. cit.*, p. 40.

were begun to be enlisted? This is an important but slightly a different issue.[33] Suffice it will be to say that the administration saw to it that only those Sikhs aught to be recruited who had the least stake in the revival or restoration of Sikh polity or an independent Khalsa order. In fact, 'the Singh recruites' were supposed to be 'Sikhs' through, and in, the British Indian army. In short, for the British the knowledge of Sikh tradition became a military need/practice.

The kind of reformed Sikhism as represented by the Nirankaris was of little use for, or danger to, the political regime yet the local administration was concerned with the reformers.[34] It will be useful to recall that Rawalpindi was original home of the Nirankaris and the region had seen an anti Nirankari agitation over the cow issue. The early Nirankaris had questioned the cow's sacredness, and the agitation against them was led by the Brahmins and Sardar Nihal Singh Chhachhi. In fact, consciously or unconsciously, the British regime and the Nirankari reformers addressed their programme to the same social constituency, namely, the relatively weaker and lower caste Sikhs who were at the prephary of the Sikh political and religious tradition. The ethical message of Guru Granth was disturbing for the forces of *status quo* such as the Brahmins and the Sardars. For this reason it came handy to the British in the pre 1857 phase. After all the Frangi had no love for the cow.[35]

No wonder, the year 1857 saw the origin of the British project of translation of the Sikh Scriptures.[36] Here, the

33. Our understanding of the British military policy as pertaining to the Sikhs is based upon George Macmunn, *The History of Sikh Pioneers* London, n.d., Appendix III.

34. See, S.S. Asoke, *Punjab Dia Lehran* (Pbi.), (Patiala, 1974), pp. 23-24.

35. The cow became a political issue after the first Anglo-Sikh War (1846). The ill-treatment of the animal caused unrest among the Lahore Hindus and Sikhs. This provocation is considered as one of the causes of the Second Anglo-Sikh War.

36. See, Proceedings, Foreign Deptt. 8th April, 1859, Numbers 141-42 (National Archives of India) to be referred as *Progds. For-Deptt.*, 8th April, 1859 (N.A.I.).

Scriptures meant both the Adi Granth and the Dassam Granth. The copies of the two Granths were supplied to the administration by the Dhirmalyia chief, Sadhu Singh Sodhi.[37] The supplied copy of the Adi Granth was the Kartarpuri Bir. This Bir had been restored to the Sodhis by the British in 1850. Before referring the translation project more, it is tempting to say a few words more about the Kartarpuri Bir.

It is true that most of the history of this Bir shrouds in mystery. Was it the original (Adi) Granth as made by Guru Arjun and Bhai Gurdass in 1604 A.D.? This is not our concern at the moment. However, its past in the 19th century is. Because it has been made as 'obscure' by a recent scholar.[38]

L.H. Griffin wrote that Sadhu Singh took the Bir to Lahore at Maharaja Ranjit Singh's request in 1830.[39] For this Sadhu Singh received the highest honour as its guardian. Griffin's reference leaves the impression that the Bir remained with the Sodhis but it enjoyed regularly the Maharaja's offerings that were fixed and specified as daily, biweekly and monthly. He further says that the Granth Sahib was always taken into the camp whenever a military expedition was undertaken.

One may add that Ranjit Singh's patronage to and faith in this Granth was no small. On May 22, 1831, Wade told Prinsep that the Maharaja sent Rupees 1100 to the Kartarpuria Granth.[40] Umdat-ut-Tawarikh show that during the 3rd week of April 1838, Nihal Singh left Kartarpur with the Granth Sahib and reached Amritsar. Kanwar Sher Singh was ordered by the Maharaja "to go forward to receive the Granth Sahib and to make an Ardas of Rs. 100".[41] We know that it was a time when Wade was pressing the Lahore to arrange a meeting of

---

37. *Ibid.*
38. W.H. McLeod, *The Evolution of the Sikh Community* (Delhi, 1976), pp. 61-62.
39. See, Harjot Oberoi, *op. cit.*, p. 112.
40. R.R. Sethi, *The Mighty and Shrewd Maharaja* (S. Chand and Company, Delhi, 1960), p. 80.
41. *Umdat-ut-Tawarikh,* Daftar III, tr., V.S. Suri (Chandigarh, 1974), p. 429.

the Maharaja with Macnaughten to chalk out a plan for intervention in Afghanistan (the Tripartite Treaty, June 1838).[42] The Sikh side had proposed Adinanagar to be the meeting place. The British wanted it to be held at Hoshiarpur. Wade was bluntly told that the place could not be of the British choice because the Maharaja would proceed to a direction "only in accordance with the order of the Granth Sahib".[43]

The Kartarpuri Bir was with the Lahore Darbar in June 1839. Refering to June 26, 1839, the Umdat-ut-Twarikh reads, "Early in the morning the Sarkar had the honour and pride of enjoying the sacred sight of Adi Granth and Baba Granth and made a prostration before them."[44]

W.H. McLeod reports that the Bir was found in the custody of Lahore court by the British after Punjab's annexation in 1849.[45] He further says that the Bir was restored to Sadhu Singh in 1850 and a copy of it was 'subsequently' presented to Queen Victoria. But he does not show either the date or purpose of this presentation. History of the 1857 translation idea can help us in this matter also.

The idea of having the Sikh Scriptures translated originated with R.N. Cust while he was in London in 1857. He was convinced that the knowledge of the Scriptures would help the British to administer the Sikhs in a better and more effective way. He did't suggest the mode of translation. This task was performed by Donald F. McLeod, his superior in the administration.[46] It was McLeod who procured the copy of the Adi Granth in the Kartarpuri Bir from Sadhu Singh. McLeod also got a copy of the Dassam Granth through Sadhu Singh. In 1859, McLeod suggested to the Govt. of India that the translation should be done in a European language and in England. However, if it was to be done in English and in

42. *Ibid.*, pp. 429-30.

43. *Ibid.*, p. 430.

44. *Ibid.*, p. 693.

45. W.H. McLeod, *The Evolution, op. cit.*, p. 62.

46. *See, Progds. For-Deptt.*, 8th April, 1859, *op. cit.*

India, the task could be assigned to R.N. Cust stationed at Amritsar. But McLeod had a preference for England. He proposed that the two Granths be presented to the Oriental library belonging to Her Majesty the Queen so that they could be translated in the first instance and studied by the orientalists after it.

Why did McLeod select Sadhu Singh? He wrote that Sadhu Singh was the chief of the Sodhi priesthood, and was, as such the representative of Guru Govind. Secondly, all the natives consulted by McLeod in this connection had "indicated him as the proper party to supply a copy as he possessed the originals written or signed by the Gurus themselves ...". Thirdly, Sadhu Singh had the means to transcribe them faithfully. Fourthly, the Sodhi had agreed to do the job.

Donald F. McLeod clearly stated that Sadhu Singh had sent him the copy 'of the Adi Granth or precepts of the first five Gurus compiled by Guru Arjan'.[47] The Bir was, said Sadhu Singh, greatly privileged one because it was 'the only true originals'. Sadhu Singh told McLeod that it was for the first time that the Sodhi had given a copy of it to any one. He had refused its copy to Maharaja Ranjit Singh. In the case of McLeod, he had agreed to supply the same "out of respect and deference to the British Government."[48] That the Sodhi was beging a recognition by the British, hinted McLeod.

Donald F. McLeod's recommendation that the Grunths be sent to England and deposited in the Queen's Oriental Library was accepted by the Govt. of India. Accordingly, the Books were sent to England "under the care of Mr. Prinsep, and a suitable Khillat was presented to the Guru"[49] *i.e.* Sodhi Sadhu Singh.

Interestingly, more reputation came the Kartarpuri Bir's way[50] when it was brought "to Patiala in 1860 to be shown to

47. *Ibid.*

48. *Ibid.*

49. See, Office Note, Govt. of Punjab, dated 8 Feb., 1872.

50. See, Harjot Oberoi, *op. cit.*, p. 112.

Maharaja Narendara Singh, who in vain tried to acquire it." The Patiala chief "fixed for its guardians a daily allowance of Rs. 51, and made them stay with their precious charge for three whole years."

It was precisely at this juncture when the Kartarpuri Bir was getting more eminence (1859-60) the Damdami Bir of the Adi Granth was choosen by a Lahore printing press in order to publish it as such. The printer and publisher was Lala Har Sukh Rai, the proprietor of the Kohinoor Printing Press, Lahore.[51] According to Piar Singh, Harsukh Rai's search for 'an authentic version of the Holy Scripture' began in 1860 A.D.[52] and the Damdami Bir was selected by him 'in consultation with Sikh High Priests at Amritsar'.[53] The publication came in A.D. 1864-65.

Piar Singh does not mention the source of his information. Nor does he spell out the names of High Priests at Amritsar. We know that Munshi Harsukh Rai had his Kohinoor Press in Lahore, and he was a printer patronized by the British since 1849.[54] Immediately after annexation, he was induced to leave Secundrabad to come to Lahore. Harsukh Rai gave to Punjab its first Urdu Newspaper. In 1864-65, the Adi Granth in the Damdama Bir was lithographed.

Be as it may, Harsukh Rai faced the question of the authenticity of Holy Granth and considered the Damdami Bir as the authentic one. A year before Harsukh Rai's search began, D.F. McLeod had accepted the Kartarpuri Bir as the original Adi Granth.[55] Both these events took place in Lahore of 1859-60. Interestingly, it was a time when Ram Singh Kuka had

---

51. Piar Singh, *Gatha Sri Adi Granth and the Controversy* (Michigan, 1996), p. 11.
52. *Ibid.*
53. *Ibid.*
54. See, Nazer Singh, *Delhi and Punjab, op. cit.*, p. 20.
55. See, *Prgds. For-Deptt.* 8th April, *1859* (N.A.I.).

started his activities in the Ludhiana region.[56] The Kukas followed the Damdami Bir and propagated it as the Granth of Guru Gobind Singh.

Adi Granth in the Damdami Bir was again lithographed in Lahore in 1868.[57] Harjot Oberoi says it was printed at Matbai Aftab Press. It was brought about by Diwan Buta Singh. We know that Diwan Buta Singh was the proprietor of the Aftab Press, Lahore and he was a great political suspect in the British eyes.[58] The police report of 1870 enlisted the Diwan as an important Kuka in Lahore because he was in touch with some of the Kuka Sants and Subas. Another British report (1871) makes him equally influential with the Lahore printing industry.

The Scriptures were not the only form of Sikh literature used by the Kukas, the Nirankaris and the Missionaries. Sakhi was equally employed. The Kukas as well as the pro-British elements invented Sakhis.[59] Whereas the followers of Ram

---

56. The police account of the Kukas (1866), says that Ram Singh started his activities in the Ludhiana area in 1858. It further says that Ram Singh assumed the title of 'Bhai' in 1860, See, *Kukian de Vithia,* p. 13, f. note.

57. See, Harjot Oberoi, *op. cit.,* p. 275.

58. See, *Kukian de Vithia,* p. 62.

59. Gur Rattan Mal popularly called Sau Sakhi has been an expression of Sikh tradition of oral history. Originating in the post Guru Gobind Singh period, it was a collection of Sakhis or stories. Some of the Sakhis were prophecies while the others were narratives about the past. Because of the penetration of present and future into the past in these Sakhis the stories were open to all kinds of influences, ideas and events.

A recent work suggest that many a stories comprising the Sau-Sakhi had their origin in the British period. Some of the stories refer to the names such as Dalip Singh and Ram Singh, See, Gurbachan Singh Nayyar, *Maokhik Itihas* (Pbi.) (New Delhi, 1990), pp. 88-89.

The police reports confirm the circulation of 'Stories' about and by the Kukas. The police had collected 'patries' written in the name of Baba Ram Singh. Interestingly, the police had reached these 'patries' through its own spies. According to Ganda Singh, Ram Singh was conscious of such communications that he considered to be the work of the Pujaris and Brahmins, See, *Kukian de Vithia,* pp. 30-31.

Singh floated stories either through the word of mouth or the circular letters about Ram Singh with a view to establish his prophethood, the British side and the police informers made stories to project the Kuka movement in particular and Ram Singh in general as a rebellious undertaking.[60] For the more enthusiastic among the Namdharis, Ram Singh was an incarnation of Guru Gobind Singh. For the more committed police informers the Kuka leader intended to restore the Khalsa raj by annihiliating the Christians. In 1866 the police confirmed the existence of 'the christian informers'. John Newton of the Ludhiana Mission sought to convince the Ambala Commissioner that the whole tendency of the Kuka reformation was to restore the power of Sikhism for the political ends.[61]

Thus by 1868, the Adi Granth, the Rahitnamas and the Sakhi had entered the Punjab public and political life by the various factors. Four prominent factors were, the Nirankaris, the Namdharis, the Christian Missions and the British administration. Each one of the factors had its own reason to employ them. Collectively, they were reviving them. Again the means and ends of the revival were different. The Adi Granth and the Janamsakhi stood printed in Lahore. By popularizing the Adi Granth in the Damdami Bir directly through their organization and indirectly by printing it, the Namdharis cleared its path to fully prevail as the Holy Granth. Coupled with the rebirth of Sakhi and more so the Janamsakhi, it made the early Sikh tradition significant socially and politically.

On the whole the political events since 1857 such as the emergence and expansion of the Nirankari and the Namdhari movements led the British regime to have an agency for information and education of the Sikhs.[62] Appearing by 1865

---

60. *Kukian de Vithia,* p. 31.

61. See, Fauja Singh Bajwa, *op. cit.,* pp. 44-47, 55, 57, 63.

62. See, Nazer Singh, 'The Khalsa Towards the Sikh Sabha', in, *Proceedings Punjab History Conference,* 1999, pp. 126-27. Also, 'Khalsa and its Modern Historians', *Journal of Sikh Studies,* Vol. xxiii, no. 1, 1999, p. 44.

the agency was comprised of D.F. McLeod, L.H. Griffin, G.W. Leitner, John Newton, Shardha Ram Philouri, E.Trumpp and Sardar Attar Singh Bhadour. All these men were engaged in three organically related activities in Punjab centred at Lahore. The activities were (1) the popularization of western education to enchance the legitimacy of British rule, (2) the creation of new literature including history-works, and (3) the creation of public opinion favourable to the British. Each one of them was closely related to the administration through either of the following organizations :

(a) the education department (est. 1858).

(b) the Ludhiana and other Christian Missions and bodies.

(c) the Anjuman-i-Punjab (est. 1865) and its allied institutes such as the Punjab Book Depot, the Oriental College and the Punjab University College.

A brief of their activities is desireable to see the making of this agency as well as its nature and functioning upto 1877, the year Trumpp published his 'The Adi Granth'.

One can begin with D.F. McLeod and L.H. Griffin for two reasons. First, the historical literature produced after 1857 can be our guide and these two persons had contributed a lot to this very literature.[63] The others who helped in producing

63. This refers to D.F. McLeod's official correspondence related to both the translation of the Sikh Scriptures Project and to the Punjab University Movement. For the translation project see his letter of Feb. 1859 in *Proceedings Foreign Department,* 8th April 1859, nos. 141-42. For the University and education, See, *Progds, Home-Education,* May 22, 1869, nos. 35-38 (N.A.I.).

L.H. Griffin published his book *The Punjab Chiefs* in 1865. The work was revised and corrected by W.L. Conran and H.D. Craik. The revised edition was published under the title *Chiefs* and *Families of Note in Punjab,* Vol. I (Lahore 1909).

Griffin's PREFACE TO THE ORIGINAL EDITION OF THE PUNJAB CHIEFS, I, is directly relevant here.

Griffin produced *The Rajas of the Punjab* in 1870. According to C.F. Massy, this book was, in a way, continuation of *the Punjab Chiefs,* See. PREFACE TO THE SECOND EDITION OF THE PUNJAB CHIEFS.

We have consulted the reprint of *The Rajas of the Punjab* published by the Punjab Language Deptt. in 1970.

this literature were Leitner, Shardha Ram through Newton and Sardar Attar Singh through Trumpp and his translation project (1869-77) under Griffin.[64]

Secondly, both McLeod and Griffin were the Punjab officials active in the Anjuman-i-Punjab movement. McLeod was associated with the Sikh Scriptures' translation project since 1859. Griffin had joined the same in 1871. Moreover, Donald McLeod was one of the two Punjab officials to participate in the Punjab Missionary conference of 1862. The other being R.N. Cust, the author of the idea of Sikh Granth's translation in 1857. Further McLeod was close to Newton and Shardha Ram while Griffin was close to Leitner and Sardar Attar Singh.

The British regime's changed attitude towards the Punjab aristocracy and the Sikh tradition was reflected as much through the educational philosophy of D.F. McLeod and G.W. Leitner[65] as the historical works of L.H. Griffin.[66]

Vaguely moddled on the Asiatic Society of Bengal, the Punjab administration organized the Anjuman-i-Punjab in 1865. The production of the vernacular literature by the western methods was the chief objective of Anjuman. Ideologically, the Anjuman was to produce a new literature to diffuse the useful knowledge. Socially, it was to be a body of the Europeans and the local aristocracy of land, trade and commerce. Its centre was Lahore, and it was presided by G.W. Leitner. Its other active European members included D.F. McLeod, C.U. Atchison and L.H. Griffin. Among its Punjabi patrons and members the prominent were the chiefs of Patiala and Nabha and Sardar Attar Singh of Bhadour.

Immediate aim of the Anjuman was the establishment of a national university in the Punjab. A sort of movement was started for this purpose in 1866, and this aim was partially

---

64. See, Nazer Singh, *History, op. cit.,* Also, *Delhi and Punjab, op. cit.,* pp. 64-74, and 'Khalsa and its Modern Historians', in *Journal of Sikh Studies,* Vol. XXIII, no. I, 1999, pp. 39-47.

65. See, Nazer Singh, *Delhi and Punjab,* pp. 68-74.

66. See, our note no. 63.

achieved with the establishment of Punjab University College, Lahore in 1869. It was McLeod's achievement, though Leitner had worked hard for the scheme. It was Leitner's belief that western education could not suceed unless it had the backing of the Priest and the Noble.[67] Likewise, McLeod was convinced that the Punjab aristocrats could be, like the emancipated serfs in Russia, a great political asset to the British provided they be associated with the administration through the educational and municipal bodies. Obviously this scheme of things assigned a new political, educational and literary role to the aristocracy including the priest and the nobel. Religious literature and the religious classes acquired a new significance and function.

D.F. McLeod desired the British administration dealing with the Sikhs to get itself acquainted with the Punjabi language and Sikh tradition. He led the Ludhiana Mission to produce a work by which the knowledge of the provincial officials learning Punjabi language could be tested.[68] The book was prepared by Shardha Ram Philouri in 1866. It was printed at the Ludhiana Mission Press in 1868. The book dealt with the life sketches of ten Sikh Gurus and an account of the Sikh kings. In addition the book contained some portions or stories from the Janamsakhi. Interestingly the book did not include the Gurmukhi grammar though it was supposed to be an educational work.[69] It was entitled as Sikhan de Raj de Vithia.

Sikhan de Vithia turned out to be an educational and evangelical work. Shardha Ram had been trained by John Newton not only in the art of printing (1859-61) at the Ludhiana Mission press but also in the method of producing the

---

67. Nazer Singh, *Delhi and Punjab,* pp. 67-68.

68. See, Henery Court (tr.), *Sikhan de Raj de Vithia* (rpt.) (Patiala, 1970), AUTHOR'S PREFACE, LXXXIV.

    It must be noted that Court published his translation in 1888 and his publication was different from the one printed in 1868. We have used court's work.

69. It was Court who added a Grammar and another portion to *Sikhan de Raj de Vithia* in 1888.

evangelical literature. Shardha Ram was both a translator and an original writer. It will be useful to recall that the Missionary conference of 1862 had adviced the missions to be familiar "with the biographies of Nanak and Govind."[70] Further, both John Newton and Donald McLeod were participants in the conference. Above all, the conference had denounced the whole later Sikh tradition by taking Guru Gobind Singh as a necessary 'evil'.

How did *Sikhan de Vithia* present the lives of Sikh Gurus and their writtings, the Scriptures? Shardha Ram had a simple but wrong view of Guru in Sikhism. He denied unity to the ten Gurus. The tenth Guru was different from Guru Nanak.[71] Guru Gobind Singh founded a new sect (the Khalsa) that was his own. Also, he had to have a Granth of his own (the Dassam Granth).[72] Before his death, the tenth Guru instructed his followers to follow 'the Granth Sahib'. In *de Vithia,* there is no reference to the guruship of Khalsa. But work records the failure of Khalsa to work without a leader for some time.[73] Hence, the question of Banda being Guru Gobind Singh's choice does't arise. The Guru's death in 1708 was so unbearable that many died after, and for, him.[74] It was Naderr that decided the Sikh religious issues in case of controversy or difference.[75]

Shardha Ram was dead sure that the theoretical evolution of 'the Granth Sahib' was complete in 1604 A.D. itself. Because Guru Arjan Dev had closed its authorship against all Gurus to come save Guru Teg Bahadur.[76] Obviously the ninth Guru had a limited chance as he was to fill merely the space left (actually allotted) for him in the Granth of 1604 A.D. Very

70. *Report of the Missionary Conference, op. cit.,* p. 267.

71. *Sikhan de Raj de Vithia,* p. 54.

72. *Ibid.,* p. 43.

73. *Ibid.,* p. 60.

74. *Ibid.,* p. 58.

75. *Ibid.*

76. *Ibid.,* p. 22.

logically the *Sikhan de Vithia* reminds how anything not written in the Granth Sahib was spurious for the Sikhs since the days of Guru Arjan.[77] Naturally, the Granth of 1604 A.D. was a bar against Guru Gobind Singh, implies *de Vithia*.

One day the tenth Guru 'took a fancy that he would send for the book of the Granth Sahib, and write something more in it'.[78] The Book was with the Sodhis of Kartarpur who refused to give it to the Guru. The Sodhis entertained a doubt about the Guru's capacity to produce a new copy of the Granth. In face of this challenge, Guru Gobind Singh was silent but not for a long time. After a few days, he discovered that 'the original Granth Ji' was no longer suited his purpose because its reading was making the Sikhs 'very feeble hearted'.[79] So the Guru "determined himself to compose such a Granth, that, from reading it, his disciples, having learnt the science of government and the use of weapons, and other kinds of expertness, should become fit for fighting."[80] Thus the Dassam Granth was produced in 1753 B.K. *i.e.* 1696 A.D.[81]

The *Sikhan de Vithia* did not employ the name 'the Adi Granth' for the book began to be made since 1604 A.D. Instead, it called it as 'the Granth Sahib'. More than once its author referred to the Dassam Granth also. The parts of Sastras were included in the Dassam Granth, he wrote. Guru Gobind Singh's 'religion was not confined to any one book or prophet or incarnation',[82] reads *de Vithia*. Yet it was upon the Granth Sahib that the tenth Guru confered Guruship before breathing the last, concluded Shardha Ram. Interestingly, the *Sikhan-de Raj de Vithia* refers to Damdama Sahib but not the Damdami Bir.[83]

---

77. *Ibid.*, p. 43.
78. *Ibid.*
79. *Ibid.*
80. *Ibid.*
81. *Ibid.*
82. *Ibid.*, p. 54.
83. *Ibid.*, p. 46.

As early as 1868, G.W. Leitner talked about the danger of Brahminical revival in the region. This he had learnt from the history of Kashmir where it was found how the Brahimanism gradually uprooted Buddhism.[84] He further said that Hinduism/Brahminism did't allow the dissenting creeds to sustain themselves for long. By implication he meant that Sikhism, a dissenting creed, faced extinction. He pointed out an other danger to religion in general. It was the exotic nature of English education system that was ruinning the classical languages, literature and educational institutions. It was demoralizing the people. Leitner wrote that the priest and the nobel stood aloof from the Government and its policies. The resultant estrangement was politically harmful to the Empire because it widened more the civilizational and racial difference between the British and the locals.

Closely following Donald McLeod and Leitner, it was L.H. Griffin who defended the Sikh nobility and tradition more directly and boldly. Between 1865 and 1870, he wrote books on the Punjab aristocracy. The first book was on the Chiefs and Families of Note in the Central and Western Punjab.[85] It was an official work to identify and enlist the erstwhile ruling class so that the administration could have a proper account of its existence and political worth.

Griffin was not writing the history of Punjab or her nobility.[86] Because he had deliberately choosen to describe only the surviving part of aristocracy. Who could have survived under the British? Obviously, the loyalists. Griffin's was an exercise in locating the sources of loyalism to the British. The rebell was not the subject of his narrative. The glorification of loyality to the Empire was Griffin's main note.

Griffin's concern for the loyalist aristocrat tended to be

84. Nazer Singh, *Delhi and Punjab, op. cit.*, p. 96

85. See, our note 63.

86. See, Griffin's PREFACE TO THE ORIGINAL EDITION OF THE PUNJAB CHIEFS.

87. See, *The Rajas of Punjab* (Patiala, 1970).

Sikh specific in his second work.[87] Outwardly, the Rajas of the Punjab was in continuation of his first book. But the Rajas had a different message too. Griffin prominently talked of 'the sikh states'.[88] He discovered the past of 'the sikh states' instructive in two ways.

First, the peaceful relationship between the Sikh Rajas in the east of Satlej and the British since the dawn of 19th century underlined only the popularity of British rule in India. Implicit here was Griffin's notion that the British empire was a common venture of the Sikhs and the British as the empire owed its formation and progress to the Sikh cooperation also.

Secondly, the history of 'the sikh states' demonstrated the constrast between the Muslim era and the British times.[89] In the 18th century the Sikh rule was established after a long drawn religious struggle against the Muslim rulers. But this religious factor came in no form the Sikh way to work out their political success under the British in the 19th century. In this Griffin indirectly suggested that Sikhism was useful to the British empire. It was borne out by the contemporary Sikh polity by which the Sikh rulers and aristocracy were actively cooperating the British administration in its derive for development and modernization through the new educational and irrigational schemes.[90]

On the whole, Griffin's work pleaded his own Government to appreciate the Sikh tradition of political loyality. To the aristocracy it assured survival. In fact a new image of the Sikh was in the making. The image took away the distinction between a Sikh nobel and a British loyalist. It is important to note that Griffin wrote at a time when the Kukas were fast spreading in and around the region under 'the sikh states' *i.e.* 1868-69.[91]

---

88. *Ibid.*, See, Griffin's PREFACE TO THE ORIGINAL EDITION OF THE PUNJAB CHIEFS.

89. *Ibid.*

90. *Ibid.*

91. *Ibid.*

E-Trumpp took his appointment as the translator of the Sikh Scriptures in November 1869. The appointment was made in London by the India office. In fact the translation project in 1857 had originated in London. Trumpp started with the translation of the Adi Granth in the Kartarpuri Bir. In October, 1870, he was supplied with the two lithographed copies of the Damdami Bir.[92] He found the lithographed copy of 1868 more clear than the one done in 1864-65. But the translator did not bother to see the difference between the Kartarpuri Bir and the Damdami Bir. His three letters written from London between 12 Feb. 1870 and 5th Oct. 1870, referred to the Granth Sahib as if it was composed of two volumes, *viz. (a)* the Adi Granth and *(b)* the Dassam Granth.[93] But one thing Trumpp had found by Feb. 1870 was that the Sacred Books of the Sikhs also covered the Rahitnamas. He took the Rahitnamas to be the works of Guru Gobind Singh. Till Oct. 1870, Trumpp was dealing with the sacred writings of the Sikhs. It will not be correct to say that he was appointed to translate the Adi Granth. It will be more wrong to say that he was appointed to translate the Holi Granth. As a matter of fact, the problem with Trumpp was that he did not consider any of the Sikh Granths with him as Holy. He took these as 'sacred' in the ordinary sense of the word sacred.

While in London Trumpp had realized the enormity of the work before him. In July 1870, he agreed to visit India so that he could get help from the Sikhs.[94] His salary was enhanced. He landed at Bombay enroute to Lahore in December 1870. How did he work in the Punjab during 1871? It is difficult to say. But the fact remains that his view of Sikh sacred writings underwent a change during the year 1871. For one thing, he continued to translate the Adi Granth but

92. See, Trumpp's Letter of 5th October 1820, quoted in Trilochan Singh, *Ernest Trumpp and W.H. McLeod.* (Chandigarh, 1994), p. 46.

93. For Trumpp's correspondence in the year 1870 see the proceedings in the Foreign Deptt. in General-A-July 1870, nos. 67-70, Nov. 1870, nos 26-27 and Dec. 1870, no. 1-2 (N.A.I.).

94. *Ibid.*

showed a greater interest in its language than its content or historical role. He continued to talk about the importance of the Dassam Granth but did not start its translation. He found his two Sikh Munshis of little use for the job.[95] Above all he began to talk of his poor health. By the close of the year 1871 he had practically postponed the translation of the Dassam Granth. Soon he abandoned it and informed the London accordingly in April 1872.[96]

How could the translator change the nature and purpose of the translation project as Trumpp did by gradually dropping the Dassam Granth? Obviously such a change was not possible without the connivance of the British authorities. Surprisingly, the Punjab administration did not raise even a single objection in this matter or any other issue such as more pay and more time demanded twice by Trumpp while in India (Sep. 1871, Dec. 1871). In fact, the Punjab authorities did not want Trumpp to be a mere translator. In other words translation for the sake of the mere progress of scholarship in Sikhism was no longer the interest of the political regime.

In early 1872, L.H. Griffin, Secretary to the Govt. of Punjab, wrote to Govt. of India that his Govt. wanted to employ Trumpp in the Oriental College, Lahore.[97] Trumpp had already threatened to abandon the translation of the Dassam Granth. Griffin expected Trumpp to help create study material in Pushto and Punjabi. Griffin and the Punjab administration failed to engage Trumpp for the new job as the translator suddenly left India in Feb. 1872. But the translation project had already been given a different orientation in and by the Lahore.

G.W. Leitner recorded that the idea of developing Punjabi as the national language of Punjab came from Trumpp. We know that the latter was superintendent of the Oriental College in 1871. Further, the teaching of Punjabi was introduced at the Oriental College by Leitner and it included the study of

95. See, *Progds For-Gen., A.* April 1872, nos. 110-114 (N.A.I.).

96. See, *Progds For-Gen., A.* May, 1872, nos. 6-9 (N.A.I.).

97. See, 'Correspondence Regarding the Retention of Dr. Trumpp's Services, in *Progds. For-Gen., A.* April 1872, nos. 110-14 (N.A.I.).

Guru Granth as well. The inclusion was justified by Griffin.[98]

Sardar Attar Singh of Bhadour was a leading and active member of the Anjuman-i-Punjab since its inception in 1865. He had a taste for Sanskrit learning. For this and his support to Govt's educational programme he was made a Senator of the Panjab University College.[99] Attar Singh was opposed to the Kukas and he had informed L.H. Griffin in 1871 that the Kukas were busy in making stories purported to give Ram Singh the image of a prophet on the model of Guru Gobind Singh. Through these stories the Sikhs were being misled to their ranks. A collection of these stories called the Sakhis were sent to Griffin by the loyal Sardar. The collection was what the tradition called as the Sau-Sakhi. In reply, the Sardar was asked to collect more such information. A copy of the Sau-Sakhi was sent to Trumpp by the administration as it was desired by Attar Singh. He had entered the good books of Griffin. Subsequently, Attar Singh translated these stories into English and these were published under the title 'the Sakhi-Book' by a Mission Press of Benaras in 1873.[100]

98. Nazer Singh, *Delhi and Punjab,* p. 124.

99. For an appreciation of Attar Singh's educational role by Griffin, See, *The Rajas of the Punjab, op. cit.,* p. 174.

100. Attar Singh Bhadour, *Sakhee Book or the Description of Guru Gobind Singh's Religion and Doctorines* (Benaras, 1873).

2 History of Sikh Scriptures' Translations : Idea Upto Trumpp

When did the Sikh Scriptures enter the british intelligence network that gradually came to be called Sikh Studies?[1] What was the nature and purpose of this network? How did it shape Sikhism and its Historiography? These are the basic questions which confront us the moment we think of India Office's Translation of Sikh Scriptures Project (1857-77) and Ernest Trumpp's English translation of the *Adi Granth* (1869-77).[2] Though it may not be possible to answer these questions perfectly in an article like this yet more than one thing about each of them can be said with certainty for there is no dearth

1. Dr. Ganda Singh was one of the first scholars to take notice of Western writers on the Sikh past in his book *Early European Accounts of the Sikhs.* However, it was with the publication of J.S. Grewal's booklet, *The Present State of Sikh Studies* (Batala, 1973) that the term Sikh Studies acquired historiographical meaning. For an early understanding of this historiographical tradition, sec, Fauja Singh, (ed.), *Historians and Historiography of the Sikhs* (New Delhi, 1978).

   Apart from Dr. Ganda Singh's book, the early European writings on the Sikhs, especially Guru Nanak, are available in parts in Guru Nanak's Birth Quincentenary Volume of the *Panjab Past and Present,* Vol. III, 1969, pp. 101-02, 105, 112, 115-17, 130, 140-41, 151-55 and 158-68. For a more handy reference, one can also have them in Darshan Singh, *Western Perspectives on the Sikh Religion* (New Delhi, 1991), Chapter II.

2. The idea of translation of Sikh Scriptures came from R.N. Cust by August 1857. In all probably the idea in 1857 originated while Cust was in London. The idea took the shape of translation project in April 1859. But the actual work on translation began only after May 1869. When was Trumpp employed for this work? The British record does not disclose it. See *Proceedings Home-Public, A,* February 1881, nos. 65-71 (N.A.I.) and *Progds., For. Gen., A,* 1873 nos. 34-37 (N.A.I.).

of evidence to enlighten our way.[3] The archival material alone is sufficient to show the ideological nature of British interest in Sikh past and literature both before and after 1849. By archival material we mean not only unpublished matter but also the official history writings/books produced by the British administrators.[4] This article is largely based upon the archival sources produced by the British regime and available in the National Archives of India, New Delhi.

At the out-set of nineteenth century John Malcolm reported the availability of Sikh Scriptures with the British scholarship of Calcutta.[5] This scholarship was comprised of Company's civil service that had its intellectual forums like the Asiatic Society of Bengal and the Fort William College.[6] He himself had the true copies of them that he consulted for making a lengthy report on the Punjab Sikhs entitled as *Sketch of the Sikhs* (1805-10). Leyden, and orientalist, helped him in this use of Sikh literature for explaining Sikh movement.

Malcolm also reported that H.T. Colebrooke, a leading Sanskritist of Calcutta too had acquired at his own the authentic versions of Sikh Scriptures.[7] Soon another Sanskritist coming from the ranks of Evangelicals in that city took a notice of Sikh literature and its language, Gurumukhi, by making an English abstract based upon *Gurbani* for the purpose of enlightening the members of the Council of Fort William

3. Besides the works of Grewal, Fauja Singh and Darshan Singh, see, Leohlin, *The Sikhs and Their Scriptures* (Lucknow, 1974) and M.A. Macauliffe, *The Sikh Religion* (New Delhi, 1978) Vol. I-VI. Also Ernest Trumpp, *The Adi Granth* or *Holy Scripture of the Sikhs* (New Delhi, 1970).
4. Hari Ram Gupta, G. Khurana and J.C. Dua had already exposed this material. See, Gupta, *History of the Sikhs* (New Delhi, 1980), Vol. III, pp. 173-309; Khurana, *British Historiography on the Sikh Power in Punjab* (New Delhi, 1985) Chapter 2, and Dua, *Eighteenth Century Punjab* (New Delhi, 1992) Chp. 2.
5. See, *The Punjab Past and Present, op. cit.*, p. 104, f. n. 1.
6. See, David Kopf, *British Orientalism and the Bengal Renaissance* (Calcutta, 1969), pp. 29, 31, 68-71.
7. *The Punjab Past and Present, op. cit.*

College.[8] He was William Carey, a Missionary Professor of 'Sanskrit and Hindoo languages' in the College of Fort William.

Obviously, the first British armed aggression against the Punjab in 1805 led to the entry of Sikh Scriptures into Sikh Studies through John Malcolm. He consciously employed *Gurbani* to explain Sikhism including the political history of punjab.[9] Doing so he gave a new meaning to Sikh past was well as a different direction to British Sikh Studies. The transformation brought about by Malcolm can be appreciated by making a brief reference to British investigations into Sikh past before 1805.

Beginning with the Delhi or Lucknow based Agents of the East India Company under Warren Hastings (1772-84) the Sikh Studies were practically diplomatic and military in their scope and concern.[10] Even the entry of *vaqanavises* or newswriters in this field by the times of Wellesley (1798-1805) did not make much change in the nature of these studies. In fact, the news writers were primarily supposed to inform Calcutta or Poona of the military or diplomatic moves of the Sikh misaldars against the Afghans, Mughals and Marathas till 1799 and against one another after Ranjit Singh's rise in Lahore.[11] In short, the British knowledge of the Sikhs upto 1805 was a matter of military-political intelligence or Akhbars and Agency Reports.

It will be useful to keep in mind that the *Akhbars* and Reports (Travelogues and newsletters) were mostly dependent for information upon Indian informers. The latter normally conducted this business of giving informations orally. Even when some of them did otherwise, they did so on the

8. 'History of Fort William College' in *Bengal Past and Present*, Vol. XXI, July-Dec., 1920, p. 184.

9. John Malcolm, *Sketch of the Sikhs* (London, 1812), pp. 3-6.

10. See, J.S. Grewal, *op. cit.*

11. For the significance of Ranjit Singh's occupation of Lahore and British reaction to it, see, *Records of the Ludhiana Agency*, P.G.R., Vol. II, Lahore, 1911, pp. 31, 136-42, 145-48.

basis of oral tradition.[12] Interview and direct observation were the chief mode of information informing early Sikh Studies. Consequently, the British writings on the Sikhs before Malcolm were practically oral histories of the Sikhs.

The British intelligence tended to reduce Sikh tradition either into a tale of militarism said to begin with Guru Gobind Singh (Hargobind) and culminating into Sikh forays (especially across Jamuna) or anti-Afghan Khalsa patriotism of the Punjab cultivators (Jats) grounded in class oppression and hatred bordering on religioracial fanaticism especially in the post Nadir Shah period.[13] The year 1739, personality of Guru Gobind Singh and secterian policy of Aurengzeb, explained Sikh political history for the early European writers. The eighteenth century made Sikh Studies. In turn, the Sikh Studies made 18th century as the story of Sikh rise against the Mughals and the Afghans. Pre-eighteenth century Sikhism and British imperialism were outside the scope of early European Sikh historiography.

However, the Holkar episode (1805) changed everything.[14] The Khalsa and the British came face to face in the Jallundhar Doab. But the Company found the Khalsa quite a friendly power ready to cooperate it against the Marathas and Afghans. Not only this, the Sikhs were more friendly to the British than to one another. The Sarbat Khalsa was no longer a military / political reality. The doctrine of Guru Khalsa

---

12. The Company Agents had their own way of writing history. They would 'employ' the Indians as their local but secret informers to collect infromation for them. The informers were equipped with the questions the Agent was interested in knowing, and they were to supply information in order to find out the answer to Agent's queries. The informer was usually asked to write down his account in Persian language, and his narrative was used by the Agent to construct Indian past in his own language and way. The oral questionnaire supplied by the Agent formed an essential and basic part of this enquiry. The dialogue between the Agent and the informer made it more oral, though it was documented.

13. See, R.N. Cust, 'The Countries between the Rivers Satlej and Jamuna', in *Linguistic and Oriental Essays* (London, 1880), Chapter I.

14. See, Nazer Singh, 'John Malcolm—A Diplomat Historian', *The Punjab Past and Present,* Vol. XXVI-II, 1992, pp. 20-35.

took a back seat. It was time for the Sikhs to be guided in all matters, stately or otherwise, by the Guru Scripture, Ranjit singh maintained retrospectively.[15] The British wished him all success by leaving Punjab to its own fate.

The increasing political importance of the institution of Guru Granth by the dawn of the 19th century was also evident from the chiefly patronage that it received for the Sikh priestly classes especially that of the Golden Temple.[16] The readers of the Scripture were given various kinds of gifts and grants including the revenue free land grants by the Sikh Sardars ever since 1973 when the House of Suckerchak made its first *dharamarth* to the Temple.[17] The emergence of Head Granthi as the 'high priest' of the Sikhs by the end of Lahore Kingdom showed only the socio-political rise of Sikh Scripture under Ranjit's rule.

With the *Adi Granth* at its centre, Golden Temple attracted the attention of every British diplomat who visted Amritsar between 1806 and 1809. John Malcolm[18], Captain Mathew[19] and Charles Matcalfs[20] suggest that the company regime should learn to appreciate the political significance of Sikh institutions and religious classes for its future dealings with the Punjab. Malcolm himself gave the lead in this direction by appreciating *Gurbani* and other, 'original Sikh authors' in his work of Sikh movement.[21] It had a great politico-ideological import for Sikhism and its future growth.

For one thing, to talk of *Gurbani* and *Vars* of Bhai Gurdas along with the *Vachittar Natak* was to talk of *Adi Granth* and Guru Nanak before Guru Gobind Singh. Without denying the

15. Sohan Lal Suri, *Umdat-Tawarikh*, Daftar II (Guru Nanak Dev University, Amritsar, 1985), pp. 69, 452.
16. *Political Proceedings*, 10 June 1853, nos. 217-220 (N.A.I.).
17. *Ibid.*
18. See, Malcolm, *op. cit.*, pp. 84-87, 118-20.
19. M.L. Ahluwalia (ed.), *Maharaja Ranjit Singh's Negotiations with the British Envoy C.T. Metcalfe* (New Delhi, 1982), pp. 94-101.
20. *Ibid.*, 412.
21. Malcolm, *op. cit.*, pp. 3-5.

significance of creation of Khalsa for the social progress (including the political rise) to Sikhs, Malcolm projected Guru Nanak as the original founder of Sikh progress as well as the author of a most appropriate method of Reformation for (19th century) India.[22] By implicity juxtapoising the path of Guru Nanak to the mission of Guru Gobind Singh, the British diplomat refused to recognize Sikh history simply as the story of activites of 18th century Khalsa. In fact, Malcolm proclaimed that the founder of Sikh movement had a promise to keep with humanity too. *Sketch of the Sikhs* delineated Guru Nanak's Mission thus.[23] 'His wish was to recall both Mohammedans and Hindus to an exclusive attention to the sublimest of all principles which inculcates devotion to God and peace towards man.'

By recognizing the usefulness of 'recall' as a subversive but legitimate subtle technique of reformation to undermine Islam and Hinduism, Malcolm actually showed that Guru Nanak could be recalled to serve the Company and the Sikhs with 'peace' and 'reconciliation'. He emphatically declared that Sikh history could be a mean of reconciliation between the Sikhs and the British.[24] His report anecdotically suggested that the 'old' Khalsa—a soldier and Zamindar—head of Punjab village—and European military officers of the Company could feel in each other's meetings as if they were 'brother' equally concerned with the security and prosperity of Punjab.[25]

As the Treaty of Amritsar (1809) made 'Sikh independence' of Ranjit Singh a British cause so Malcolm thought it proper to make Sikh history as a British Indian public concern. He refused to judge Guru Nanak and Sikhism by Sikh political rise alone. In fact, he advised others too not to do it so.[26] More positively speaking, he suggested that a final judgement on the genesis of Sikh movement should be passed only after

22. *Ibid.*, pp. 152-73, 187-88.

23. *Ibid.*, p. 23.

24. *Ibid.*, pp. 5-6, 23, 144-45.

25. Nazer Singh, 'More on Malcolm' in *Proceedings Punjab History Conference,* (1994).

26. Malcolm, *op. cit.*, pp. 23-24.

deciphering Guru Nanak's *bani.* He recommended that the *Adi Granth* should be partially translated to compile an authentic biography of the founder of Sikhism.[27]

Malcolm was sure that such a biography of Guru Nanak would enlighten (the Evangelical and Benthamite radical) reformers to see the need indigenize their reform techniques by transforming them in the light of the experience of Guru Nanak of the *Adi Granth.* In short, he made early Sikhism significant for British India. In this way, he authenticated its originality or Indianness and also established *Gurbani* as an historical literature to reconstruct a new reformation for 19th century India.

J.D. Cunningham upheld Malcolm's judgement on the character of Guru Nanak's message and its contemporary relevance.[28] More than once, he quoted the *Adi Granth* to show how the Guru conceived God as Truth beyond rituals and secterian worship of 'the Moolla, and the Pandits, the Darvesh and the Soonyassee'.[29] For Cunningham, Guru Nanak was the only one among the medieval reformers of India 'to perceive the true principles of reform'.[30] In fact, the Guru's search for truth was the same as that of 'Plato, Bacon, Descartes and Alghazali'.[31] Yet the essence of his teachings was not different from 'the philosophy of his countrymen'.[32] For Cunningham, Sikhism was the consumation of Islam and Hinduism. On this very account, its political growth towards nationality was remarkably, unique but Indian event for it was an indigenous development in the first instance.

Secondly, Cunningham emphatically declared that Sikhism was a living religion. By it he implied that there was no need for Punjab to import reformation either from Europe or British India. He did not see much difference between Christianity, Sikhism and the teachings of Ram Mohan Roy.

27. *Ibid.*, p. 22.

28. *The Punjab Past and Present, op. cit.*, pp. 151, 153-54.

29. *Ibid.*, p. 152.

30. *Ibid.*, p. 151.

31. *Ibid.*, p. 152.

32. *Ibid.*, p. 153.

By projecting Guru Nanak as an ally of the modern reformers, Malcolm and Cunningham led the British administrators, especially those who were under the impact of Orientalism and Evangelicalism to be attentive to Sikh tradition. H.H. Wilson, the leading Sanskritist, translated some passages in the *Adi Granth* to show the Hindu civilizational background of Sikh worship at Benaras.[33] But more than Wilson, it was Robert Needham Cust who underlined the Indian character of Guru Nanak's reformation.[34] However, Cust denied Cunningham's claim that Sikhism was a living religion any more.[35] It simply meant that Guru Nanak's message could not be a principle of Indian reformation under the British. Yet Cust was all for making a proper understanding of Sikhism for British political and religious interests.

Cust was an important Punjab administrator known for his Evangelical ideas.[36] He was a strong supporter of John Lawrence's 'Christian Policy' which was in the making by 1857.[37] One of the essentials of this policy was the use of religion, Christianity, to enhance the moral legitimacy of British rule by giving it a 'religious look' for the Indian eye. For this, it interpreted the state principle of religious neutrality to mean that Christianity be given a free hand to grow in India so the Empire could be saved from the Hindu and Muslim fanaticism—which was supposed flourished on the mistaken Indian belief that the British were irreligious rulers.

33. H.H. Wilson, 'A Sketch of the Religious Sects of the Hindus', *Asiatic Researches,* Vol. XVII, 1832, pp. 231-39.

34. Cust took a note of Guru nanak as early as 1846 when he wrote an article on the countries between Satlej and Jamuna. But it was in 1859 that he compiled what may be called the first truely historical life sketch of the Guru. A copy of this 'pamphlet' was sent to the Secretary of State for India. The 'pamphlet' was reprinted in 1874 and 1881. In the version of 1881, it was entitled 'Guru Nanak The Indian Reformer'. For this version, see, *The Punjab Past and Present, op. cit.,* pp. 158-68.

35. *Ibid.,* p. 166.

36. R.N. Cust, *Memories of Past Years of a Septuagenarian* (London, 1899) *passim.*

37. See, Charles Aitchison, *Lord Lawrence and the Reconstruction of India Under the British* (Oxford, 1916), pp. 119-20.

The conversion to Christianity was in no way impolitic was clear from Dalip Singh's change of religion soon after the Punjab's annexation. So when the Evangelical quarters raised the salogan 'Christianity best consolidates the empire' in badly shaken India of 1857, the Punjab regime appreciated it by suggesting that lower caste men, especially the Mazahbis, might be recruited to the British army with a view and intention of possibly making them soldiers of the Cross. John Lawrence recommended the raising of, Mazahbi and Christian regiments'.[38] Some such regiments were actually raised. This entry of lower caste and class Sikhs (or Hindus) in the army during 1857-58 led the Evangelicals to hope that Sikh tradition could be subverted for British military/political and Christian religious purposes.

The year 1857 definitely threw up the question of definition of Sikhism. Cust conceived the idea of translation of Sikh scriptures.[39] He was in London when the uprising broke out. Back in India, he consulted D.F. Mcleod, an other pro-Evangelist Punjab official, in this connection.[40] The two together agreed that Sikh Scriptures should be translated either into a European language or Hindostani[41] to bridge the gap between the Sikhs and administration. Cust himself volunteered to undertake this job provided he was given permission and necessary funds for it.[42]

It is important to note that it was also a time (1859) when Cust practically opposed the British policy of patronizing Golden Temple.[43] As a Commissioner of Amritsar, he unsuccessfully disassociated the British administration from

---

38. See, George Macmunn, *The History of Sikh Pioneers* (London, n.d.) Appendix III.
39. See note 2.
40. *Proceedings Foreign Deptt.*, 8 April 1859, nos. 141-42 (N.A.I.).
41. R.N. Cust, 'The Adi Granth, or The Sacred Book of The Sikhs. By Dr. Ernest Trumpp, *Linguistic and Oriental Essays* (London, 1891), p. 262.
42. Proceedings, 8 April, 1859, *op. cit.*
43. See Nazer Singh, 'Early British Attitude Towards the Golden Temple', *Journal of Regional History*, Vol. III, 1982, pp. 90-91.

the management of Amritsar Temple on the ground that the principle of religious neturality did not permit the state officials to preserve the heathen religious institutions. In the case of Golden Temple, the official disassociation was more desirable because to maintain this Temple was to save the fast dying Khalsa polity, wrote he.[44]

The preservation of traditional Sikhism was not the purpose of Cust when he recommended translation of Sikh Scriptures in the same way as John Lawrence's objective in creating Mazhabi regiments was not to strengthen sikh material tradition for the sake of Khalsa. The lower caste and partial sikhs were enlisted in the British army to undermine the social base of Khalsa polity. The translation of the Scripture was expected to undermine the ideological base of Khalsa.

Cust was aware of the significance of translation as a mode of recreating a tradition. The translation of Bible had led to a revolution in christianity, he reminded the world.[45] In order to demonstrate it in the case of Sikhism, the Amritsar Commissioner composed a life sketch of Guru Nanak in 1859. Later on, it was entitled 'Guru Nanak the Indian Reformer'[46] Cust's account of Guru Nanak was the one "from which all the marvellous has been excluded, and which Hindu, Mahometan, and Christian can take credit."[47]

Cust's Guru Nanak was for the non-Sikhs. The Guru laboured "to break through the tyranny of priest craft, rituals and caste."[48] Moreover, he "tride to amalgamate the Hindu and Mahometan religions, and convince all, that they were really brothers, descended from one father."[49] Above all, cust did not see Guru Nanak as a Sodhi or Bedi for his message "gave no authority to his descendants to practize the wicked

44. *Ibid.*

45. R.N. Cust's letter dated 2 May 1872, in *Proceedings Foreign, General, A, Feb., 1873,* no. 64 (N.A.I.).

46. See note 34.

47. *The Punjab Past and Present, op. cit.*, pp. 167-68.

48. *Ibid.*, p. 158.

49. *Ibid.*

custom of killing their daughters."[50]

The British reform of Sikh people and religion had begun with Cust who found the 19th century Sikhs much deviated from the original percepts of their religion. They did not fulfil the intentions of Guru Nanak, Cust declared. In fact, the Guru stood betrayed both by the Sikhs and other 'thousands of his countrymen'.[51] Cust noted how the Punjabis lived by the memory of Guru Nanak but "do not attend to his words.[52]" Cust, the Amritsar Commissioner, reported in 1859 that Sikhism had no future.[53] By denying a future to Sikhism, Cust raised the question of fulfillment of Guru Nanak's mission through British rule and Christianity. He assigned the West the task of appropriating the Guru's word, *Gurbani*. Translation was a means of this appropriation.

But translation was only the beginning of the process of appropriation.[54] The process itself was to be a long drawn one. Moreover, it was to be completed without much controversy. Further, it was never to be a one man show. The western scholarship was to be associated with it. The translation was to induce them to come forward for this undertaking. As the debate and controversy was to be avoid for tactical reasons so there was no need for the translator to raise any theological issue.[55] He was only to help in arming the scholar-reformers by placing at their proposal the first hand information in shape of translated *Gurbani* to make the Sikhs "see how much they have deviated from the example and percepts of their great Teacher."[56]

Unfortunately for the British, the project failed at the take-off stage. Trumpp is said to be individually responsible for this failure. His missionary background/methodology and ill-

50. *Ibid.*, p. 162.

51. *Ibid.*, p. 167.

52. *Ibid.*

53. *Ibid.*, p. 166.

54. See R.N. Cust's letter dated 2 May 1872, *op. cit.*

55. *Ibid.*

56. *The Punjab Past and Present*, p. 168.

health are enlisted as factors to explain it by his critics.[57] All this may be true, but what is more significant is the fact that the first critics of Trumpp were the British themselves, and these crities were none other than the original authors of the idea of translation of Sikh Scriptures, namely, Cust[58] and McLeod.[59]

Both Cust and McLeod found Trumpp's method faulty. They said that he killed the project by pre-maturally exposing Sikh tradition to unnecessary theological condemnation. In this way, the translator confused means with the ends. His job was to make a plain translation. Instead, he passed theological judgements against Sikhism.[60]

Surprisingly, the Sikh critics of Trumpp also see his missionary spirit as largely responsible for producing an anti-Sikh translation. It is a fact that he did not conceal the true *i.e.* Evangelical nature of either his own being or of his work. He approached Sikh tradition in the most traditional missionary way. He did not know as to how the Evangelical objectives could be achieved in a non-missionary way—as it was being demanded from him. But one must realize the translation project would have been in no way less Evangelical without trumpp or with a different trumpp.

It will be equally superfluous to emphasize his German background or linguistic approach while determining the objectives of the Project.[61] The project was a state undertaking. Its destiny was not be determined by Trumpp alone. Equally important is the fact that the nature of British interest in the project underwent an important modification by a decade after its origin.

In 1872, Cust and McLeod told London authorities that

57. R.N. Cust, 'Dr. Trumpp', *Linguistic and Oriental Essays*, Vol. I (London, 1898), pp. 143-45.

58. Cust's Letter dt. 2 May, 1872, *op. cit.*

59. McLeod's Letter in *Proceedings Foreign General, A,* Feb. 1873, nos. 58-67.

60. See, N.G. Barrier's Article in Fauja Singh, *op. cit.*, pp. 166-185.

61. *Ibid.*

the translation project had missed its real aim.[62] But Trumpp alone was not responsible for this disorientation. The Punjab administration had also gone astray from the original scheme.[63]

Cust reminded the British that the translator was never supposed to show the theological, linguistic or political value of Sikh Scriptures. He expressed doubt about Trumpp's linguistic competence by pointing out that the German Doctor's notion of the language of *Adi Granth* as old and absolete Gurmukhi was philologically hardly tenable.[64] There was nothing like old Gurmukhi or new Gurmukhi, wrote Cust.

Cust and McLeod also did not concur in Trumpp's view that there was no one in India to help the translator by making the Scriptures intelligible to him through commentaries. Both Sikhs and non-Sikhs understood the Scriptures well and Trumpp could have their assistance, asserted McLeod.[65]

But these arguments of Cust and McLeod were comprehended neither by Trumpp nor by the Punjab regime. Trumpp said that he was unable to draw a line between a translator and interpretor as demanded by McLeod.[66] The Lahore could not appreciate McLeod's notion of 'popularized translation' because it wanted Trumpp's Translation to be of some use for its policy towards the Namdharies *i.e.* Kukas. The Punjab officials during 1871-73 were interested in knowing the scriptural basis of Sikh polity which the Kukas were determined to revive. Trumpp had to demonstrate the political worth of his project. He did so by denying originality to Sikh theology. He also performed this task by ignoring the *Dassam Granth*.[67] To ignore *Dassam Granth* was to ignore Sikh policy or war culture. It made Kukaism more artificial. Trumpp's translation of *Adi Granth* raised the question : who were the Kukas?

---

62. Cust's Letter and McLeod's letter dt. 3 May, 1872, in *Proceedings Forg. Gen., A,* Feb., 1873, nos. 58-67 (N.A.I.).

64. Cust's Letter, *op. cit.*

65. McLeod's Letter, *op. cit.*

66. See 'Office Note' made by Punjab Govt., dt. 8 Feb., 1872, in *Proceedings Foreign General,* A, April 1870, nos. 110-114 (N.A.I.).

67. Trumpp's Letter dated 12 April, 1872 to Under Secretary of State for India in *Proceedings Foreign General, A,* Feb. 1873, no. 59 (N.A.I.).

3 The Idea Under Trumpp

The British Sikh studies entered a new phase in 1869 with the beginning of English translation of Sikh holy book, the Adi Granth, by E. Trumpp. In fact, the Adi Granth in Kartarpuri Bir and the Dassam Granth had been sent to England in 1859 and these two books were to be translated into a European language. The translation idea had originated with R.N. Cust in London in the wake of eruption of the uprising of 1857. The Court of Directors had approved it in August 1857. However, nothing was heard of this undertaking till May, 1869 when the Punjab administration "suggested that the enquiry be made whether anything had been done towards their translation".[1] It was found that a translator was yet to be appointed. Showing a deep interest in the matter, the Lahore "suggested to the Home government that, if it was found impossible to have it done in England, the translation should be made here."[2]

Made in July 1869, the Punjab's second suggestion led the London authorities to act swiftly in the matter. It did not hand over the project to the Punjab administration. But they found the translator in E. Trumpp. Trumpp's appointment was for four years from November 1869. Out of these first three years were to be spent on in Europe while the rest of his tenure was for work in India 'if he found it necessary'. For his European stay he was to draw a salary of £ 300 per annum where as in India he was to be paid £ 500 from November 1,1872.[3]

---

1. See *Proceedings Foreign-General, A.* July 1869, nos. 68-69, N.A.I to be referred as *Progds. For-Gen., A.*

2 . *Ibid.*

3 . See *Progds. For-Gen., A,* Sep.1873, *nos. 6-10.*

Why was the Punjab administration so much interested in the Sikh scriptures in 1869? The question cannot be answered directly. But a few circumstances need to be noted. The British concern for the *bani* and life of Guru Nanak was as old as John Malcolm's report of 1805-10 (Sketch of the Sikhs). It had considerably increased as shown by the works of Murray-Bhangu and J.D. Cunningham in the 1840's. The use of Sikh holy writings by both the Christian Missions in league with the British administrators (like R.N. Cust and Donald McLeod) and by the rising Kuka movement under Baba Ram Singh, the Namdhari, was on the increase since 1863.[4] In search of a new Sikhism, the reformers—the western (the administrators and the Missionaries) as well as the indigenous (the Namdharis) were falling upon the scriptures. The political regime was unlikely to fail in noticing the political significance of Gurbani after the circulation of Baba Ram Singh's *circulars* advising his followers 'to sing the Granth together' and 'be afraid of none'.[5] Interestingly, the police reports on the Kukas for the years 1867 and 1868 were careful to notice as to how well versed was Baba Ram Singh with 'the Granth of Guru Gobind Singh :[6]

We know that by 1868, the Damdama Bir of the Adi Granth stood printed in Lahore. Further, the year 1868 also saw the publication of Shardha Ram Philouri's book *Sikhan de Raj de Vithia* by the Ludhiana Mission.[7] The *Vithia* was dedicated to Donald McLeod—the man who had recommended in 1859 that the Sikh Scriptures be translated by a European scholar, and in England. It shall be useful to keep in mind that it was John Newton of the Ludhiana Mission who had told the Punjab

4. See, Nazer Singh, 'The Khalsa Towards the Singh Sabha' in *Proceedings Punjab History Conference,* 1999, pp. 126-27.

5. See, Ganda Singh, *Kukian de Raj de Vithia* (Patiala, 1990), p. 15. Also, Fauja Singh, *Kuka Movement* (Delhi, 1965), pp. 44-63.

6. Ganda Singh says that by 'the Granth of Guru Gobind Singh' the British record meant the Adi Granth in the Damdama Bir, See, *Kukian de Vithia,* p. 15.

7. See, Nazer Singh, 'Khalsa and its Modern Historians' in, *Journal of Sikh Studies,* Vol. XXIII, no. I, 1999, p. 46, note 32.

administration in 1863 that there was nothing religious about Baba Ram Singh's movement. The Kuka movement in 1866 stood, said R.G. Taylor, in the words of Newton, for 'the revival of the Khalsa with political ends'.[8] On the whole, the police were trying to distinguish Baba Ram Singh from his followers by describing him as a reformer, though his organization was drifting towards revivalism. Baba Ram Singh's reformation was based upon the scriptures. But this reformation was becoming more and more 'the revival of Khalsa' at the hands of his followers grounded in, and moved by, the Sakhis of Guru Gobind Singh and Khalsa. It was this pecularity of the Namdhari movement that might have led the Punjab Govt. To get at its disposal the translated Sikh scriptures so that it could meet this political situation more effectively.

Be as it may, Trumpp wrote to the London officials in May 1870 that his work was difficult.[9] One difficulty was the language of the books. The second was his failure to see the enormousness of the work in hand. He pleaded for an increase in his salary and other changes in the terms and conditions of his service. In July 1870, he entered into a new agreement with the London. By the new deal, the translator was to proceed to India at the earliest possible.[10] He was to get a salary of £ 500 per annum for the first year, and £ 400 for the second one. In India, Trumpp was to receive the help of 'two competent Sikh Moonshis'. But his total expenses and tenure were in no case to exceed £ 1850 and five years, respectively.

Trumpp landed at Bombay on December 10, 1870. From there he came to Lahore.[11] How did he work in Punjab during 1871? It is not possible to say. But two preliminaries can be

---

8 . Quoted in Fauja Singh Bajwa, *op. cit.*, p. 57. Also, *Gooroo Ram Singh and the Kuka Sikhs,* compiled by Nahar Singh (New Delhi, 1965, p. 18.

9 . See, *Progds. For-Gen.*, A. July 1870, nos. 67-70.

10 . See, *Progds. For-Gen.*, A. Nov. 1870 nos. 26-27.

11 . See, *Progds. For-Gen., A.* April, 1872, nos. 110-14. Also, *Progds. For-Gen., A.* May 1872, nos. 6-9.

made quickly about his conception of Sikh scriptures. First, he regarded the Sikh books 'holy' in the ordinary sense of the word. Secondly, it was in Lahore that he had more clearly found that 'the sacred books of the Sikhs' were not confined to Adi Granth and Dassam Granth. These also included the Rehatnamas of Bhai Nand Lal and Prehlad. He took these two Rehitnamas as the work of Guru Gobind Singh. Where did he have the fascination about the Rahitnamas from? It is not clear. Trumpp looked upon the Adi Granth as 'the Chief sacred book of the Sikhs'. For him the Dassam Granth was also 'the Granth Sahib'. He called it 'the second sacred book of the Sikhs'. Throughout the year 1870 Trumpp regarded the Dassam Granth relevant to a proper understanding of Sikhism. But he changed his view about the Dassam Granth while he was in India during 1871. Why did this change?

In his letter of April 25, 1871, Trumpp told the Government that he was unable to rely upon the aid and advice of the Sikh granthis 'as none of them had the slightest knowledge of their grammar'.[12] The Adi Granth was written in 'the old Punjabi' that comprised of a number of dialects of north India between Sindh and Bihar. He described the book as 'very poor literary composition'. But he showed a considerable interest in the language and grammar of the Adi Granth. The translator was sure that 'Indian philologists would be surprised when they see the grammar of the Granth'.

Going by his letter of 25th April, Trumpp was over taken by the grammarian and cleric in him. He expressed his inability to complete the translation within two years. He did not say anything about the Dassam Granth. Obviously, its translation was yet to start.

In September 1871, Trumpp once again asked for an increase in his salary from £ 400 to £ 500.[13] In addition to it he demanded an allowance of Rupees 200 to meet his expenses for his Simla stay during the summer months. He talked of high cost of living in India and threatened to 'throw up his

12 . See, *Progds. For-Gen., A,* April 1872, nos. 110-14.

13 . *Ibid.* Also, *For-Gen, A,* May 1872, nos. 6-9.

appointment and return to England'. He reminded the administration that the Dassam Granth was yet to be translated, and it was 'the Granth of Govind Singh' which "throws considerable light on the political principles and constitution of the Khalsa Sikhs."[14] By highlighting the political importance of the Dassam Granth, Trumpp was underlining the political worth and nature of his undertaking in Lahore.

The translators September demands were accepted by the British regime in December 1871.[15] Even this did not satisfy him. Soon the Punjab Government "reported his resignation and withdrawl from the translation of the Granth of Govind Singh unless... that two years were allowed him to elaborate its translation in England on a salary of £ 300 per annum in addition to the one year allowed him for its preparation here, and the two and a half allowed for the elaboration of the Adi Granth."[16] This Punjab report was based on Trumpp's letter of 30th December 1871 in which he had once again threatened 'to leave India by the end of February 1872'.

Surprisingly, the Punjab report admitted that Trumpp's threat came a few days 'after he received the sanction' to his September demands. More surprisingly, the Lahore was willing to go to any extent to keep his services with itself. In fact, by the beginning of 1872 the translator and the Punjab administration had entered into a different kind of relationship. The translation of the Dassam Granth was no longer on their agenda. No more was Trumpp a mere translator of the Sikh Scriptures.

As to the Punjab regime, its officiating Secretary, L.H. Griffin, endorsed Trumpp's 'unwillingness' to work on the Dassam Granth. It was on January 11, 1872. Griffin asked more time for Trumpp in Punjab. Why was the Lahore so keen to have him for a longer period? It was because he was found more useful in ways other than the translation. Griffin had

14 . *Ibid.*

15 . *Ibid.*

16 . *Ibid.*

decided to employ Trumpp in and for the Punjab Government and her educo-political schemes. Griffin's letter reads :[17]

> We are very anxious to keep Dr. Trumpp, who is a most valuable man, and were hoping to be able to utilize him as a Pushto Professor, of which language he is one of the best living authorities.

By the end of January 1872, the Punjab administration made a plan to ensure the translator's stay in Lahore. On January 29, the Punjab reported that Trumpp might be employed by it in the following way :[18]

1. During 1872 Trumpp would act as a translator as well as Superintendent of the Oriental School, Lahore. He was to be Lecturer in Sanskrit, Prakrit, Persian and Pushto. For it he was to get an additional allowance of rupees 300 per month.
2. From January 1873 to December 1874 he was to 'work out the translation' on a salary of £ 300 per annum.
3. He was entitled to a three month leave during the hot months 'to spare his health for the translation'.

But the Punjab offer did not completely satisfy Trumpp. He made a fresh application asking a salary for himself that was 'not to be less than £ 700 per mensem' whatever might be its source'.[19] This was readily accepted by the Lahore. Forwarding Trumpp's one more application on February 8, 1872, Griffin observed :[20]

> His Honour purposes to utilize him for Pushto and Punjabi lectures and examinations, that the preparation of improved mannuals of those languages, while he can also be engaged as Sanskrit lecturer at the University College.

Interestingly, Griffin also reported that Trumpp had

17 . *Ibid.*

18 . *Ibid.*

19 . *Ibid.*

20 . *Ibid.*

'completed his preparation for the full translation of the Adi Granth in one year, instead of the two allowed him'.[21] How was this feat performed? Both Trumpp and Griffin were silent. Obviously, the translation of the two Granths was no longer a primary concern of the administration as well as of the translator by February 1872.

While the Calcutta and London officials were deliberating over the Punjab proposals, Trumpp left India. He did not respond positively to Griffin's 'urgent remonstrances'.[22]

Griffin's intentions or the Punjab administrations' apparently educational and intellectual plans at the dawn of 1872 as evident from Griffin's letter of Feb. 8 should be our concern to the extent they shaped a new context for the translation project. In fact the project was no longer a translation undertaking as it was conceived during 1857-59 by R.N. Cust and Donald McLeod. The undertaking stood yolked to yield cultural and political results such as the reform and revival of Sikh history, literature and Punjabi language with a view to take winds out of the Kuka sails and to sharpen the boundaries of Sikhism vis-a-vis Hinduism.

We know that in December 1871, Griffin was informed as to how Baba Ram Singh had invented for himself a prophethood on the pattern of Guru Gobind Singh through the sakhis popularized by the Kuka preachers. The informer was Sardar Attar Singh Bhadour, and he was asked to gather more information about the Kukas and also to keep watch on them. In this way was originated Attar Singh's work 'the Sakhee-Book'.[23] Needless to say that this collection of sakhis was hailed by its compiler as 'the Discriptions of Guru Gobind Singh's Religion and Doctorines', and the work was published at a Mission Press in Benaras in 1873. For Attar Singh, the chief cause of violent Kuka out-break in 1871 was these sakhis confusing the Kukas and the Khalsa for the ignorant Sikhs or

21 . *Ibid.*

22 . See, L.H. Griffin, *Ranjit Singh* (rpt.), Delhi, 1967, pp. 39-40.

23 . See, Attar Singh Bhadour, *Sakeei Book* or *the Discriptions of Guru Gobind Singh's Religion* and *Doctorines* (Benaras, 1873), PREFACE.

the followers of Baba Ram Singh. Trumpp had already pointed out the ignorance of the Sikh elite (gyanis) about the Sikh scriptures. Seen in this light, 'Sikh ignorances about their own tradition/past had become a current religious and political issue. The political establishment sought itself to address to this issue by arranging a modern Sikh education having the positive interest in Scriptures as its part and the Gurmukhi its medium. It was a time when the idea of developing Punjabi as 'the national language' of Punjab came from Trumpp. It may be further useful to keep in mind that Griffin himself had produced a two volume work (1865, 1870)[24] on the Punjab and Sikh aristocracy to enlist it in favour of the British by showing that there was no religious conflict between Sikhism and the British rule as it was evident from the past of Sikh states in the cis-satlej areas.[25] Attar Singh was already on the Senate of the Punjab University College. In short Trumpp's stay in Punjab could't and was not as barren as made out by his critics since Macauliffe.[26]

24 . See, Nazer Singh, *'Khalsa and Its Modern Historians', op. cit.*, pp. 42-43, notes, 33, 35, 44.

25 . *Ibid.*

26 . Macauliff's first lecture on 'the Sikh Religion' given in 1903 at Simla devotes a paragraph to Trumpp. The para is full of statements about the translation project and the translator. The very first statement is not only value loaded against Trumpp but is also factually incorrect. It reads 'The only writer who undertook to give a full account of the Sikh religion was Dr. Trumpp, a German Missionary employed by the India office to translate the Adi Granth'. This statement is followed by an anecdote about Trumpp in Amritsar. His meeting with the Sikh scholars is shown as ending 'by his pulling out a cigar case and perfuming the Granth Sahib, which lay before him on the table, with tobacco somke.' The incident is used to explain Trumpp's failure to have cooperation from the Sikh *gyanies.* This failure, in turn, led the translator to take 'the Adi Granth to Munich with him, and there, aided by the German genius of Industry, produced what be considered a translation of it.' Only a divine mind could follow his translation, said Macauliffe. He also approved the Sikh memorial to the Viceroy against the translation and told his Simla audience how the Sikhs took the translation as 'an standing insult' to themselves.

(Contd.)

True that Trumpp did not directly participate in the British educational and practical schemes for the Sikhs by leaving Lahore suddenly. Yet he could not and did not fail to involve himself with the contemporary issues before the Sikhs and their religion. In fact, he had a strong desire to tell the world something new about Punjabi. Also he had learnt something about the Sikh tradition in Lahore.

Within less than two months of his departure from Lahore for Germany, Trumpp informed the London authorities that he had no wish to translate the whole Dassam Granth. His letter of April 12, 1872, said that the translation of the entire Granth of Guru Gobind Singh would be 'more or less a useless undertaking'. It was, he said, because the book was popular with a small section of Sikhs called the Singhs or the following of Guru Gobind Singh. He suggested that it would be proper to translate 'the four books of Gobind Singh' *i.e.* Guru Gobind Singh's own four works in the Dassam Granth.[27] He was further of the view that the Rahitnamas were equally important keys to the constitution of Khalsa, and these might be translated. Obviously, the translator in Lahore was not without good advisors.

Who were the advisors of Trumpp in Lahore or Punjab?

(Contd.)

Macauliffe clearly said that he wanted the British to discard Trumpp's translation.

Macauliffe's account of Trumpp and the translation project in this paragraph can be easily shown to be half truth. First, Trumpp was not employed to translate the Adi Granth. Nor was the translation project in 1859 or 1869, confined to the Adi Granth and its translation. In 1877 also Trumpp and India office did not produce only the translation of Adi Granth. Secondly, the Amritsar ancedote may or may not be true. But even if true, it was in no way connected with Trumpp's departure from Lahore in early 1872. How did it matter that Trumpp worked on the translation in Munich also? or How did it matter that the translator was a 'German'? Macauliffe was too much presumptous. See, *The Sikh Religion A Symposium* (Calcutta, 1958), pp. 1-2.

27. See, *Progds. For-Gen., A,* May 1872, nos. 6-9.

How did he actually work in India? These questions cannot be answered directly at the moment. But the British record concedes that there was a kind of 'sikh Committee' to guide him.[28] C. Pearson, an official in the Punjab education department confessed that he had met the translator in Lahore inconnection with the translation of the Dassam Granth.[29] Griffin's presence in Lahore and his interest in Sikh history, education and the translator we have already seen.[30] The very fact that the Lahore was in 1869 ready, in case England was to fail, to handle the translation project directly showed that Punjab was well prepared for the event. We know that the Punjab missions had a clear preference for Guru Nanak over Guru Gobind Singh, and for the Adi Granth over the Dassam Granth. Little wonder if Trumpp showed no real interest in the Dassam Granth. After all he was not stanger either in Punjab or to the Missionaries. The Mission men like John Newton had a commanding influence with the education officials.

In April 1872, Trumpp gave reasons for discarding the Dassam Granth and there by reducing the scope of translation project from a scheme for translating the two Sikh scriptures into an undertaking for the translation of only the Adi Granth. He justified his step on the following grounds :[31]

A. The Dassam Granth save the four books of Guru Gobind Singh contained nothing 'but translations from Purans' and these translations "throws no light whatever on the Sikh religion as such".

B. The Granth was a complicated work, difficult to be handled by a physically weak and financially hard pressed man like the translator.

28. See, Cust's letter dt. 2 May, 1872 in *Progds. For-Gen.*, A, Feb. 1873, no. 63.

29. C. Pearson to T.H. Thonton, dt. 30 June, 1873, in *Progds. For-Gen., A,* Sep. 1873, no. 7.

30. See, Nazer Singh, 'Khalsa and Its Modern Historians', *op. cit.*

31. See, *Progds. For-Gen., A,* May 1872, nos. 6-9 and Also, *Progds For-Gen., A,* Feb. 1873, no. 59.

C. No translator could translate the book in a single go. It could be done successively, one after the other and not at once.

D. One could well begin with the Rahitnamas.

E. Trumpp would in no case agree to work for the translation of whole Dassam Granth. The Govt. was free to choose another translator for this task.

The Secretary of the State for India to whom were made the above proposals by Trumpp sought the advice of Donald McLeod, R.N. Cust and A. Grote.[32] We know that Cust and McLeod were the original authors of the translation project. The replies of all these three reached the India office in May 3, 1872. While Grote agreed with Trumpp in totality, the other two gentlemen disapproved Trumpp's method and rejected his conclusions about the Granths or the nature of Sikh literature in general.

Cust and McLeod asked the London authorities not to abandon the Dassam Granth for the book was associated with the political tradition of the Sikhs. They advised that Trumpp should be relieved of his duty of translating the Dassam Granth. Further, the Punjab Government should be directed to get this book translated by a team of scholars that might include the two top officials of her education department, an English educated Hindu Munshi, and some Sikh readers of the Granth from Lahore and Amritsar. The translation team must be headed by a European. McLeod spelled out the names of the Europeans and the Hindu. The Europeans were captain Holyrod and C. Pearson. The Hindu was Bihari Lal Puri.[33] Cust drew attention to a 1868 translation of 'some portions of the Adi Granth by Pandit Shardha Ram at Ludhiana'.[34]

As to the method and quality of Trumpp's translation of

32. For this correspondence See, *Progds. For-Gen., A,* Feb. 1873 nos. 58-63 (N.A.I.).

33. See, Donald McLeod's Letter dt. May 3,1872, in *Progds. For-Gen., A,* Feb. 1873, nos. 58-63.

34. Cust's Letter in *Progds., Ibid.*

the Adi Granth, McLeod expressed great dissatisfaction. The translator's technique of explanning translation by his 'notes' was the least desireable in McLeod's view.[35] Implicit in McLeod's argument was the truth that through his 'notes' Trumpp had entered the Sikh scriptures to expose them to modern Philological and Christian criticism. In this process the translator failed to see the positive link between Sikh literature and the Sikh way of life both in the past and present, said McLeod. The translation project was, recalled McLeod, conceived in 1859 as a long term plan for producing a European and modern scholarship in Sikhism supposed to mediate between the empire and the Sikhs so that the two could be more useful to each other. For McLeod, Trumpp was an utter failure in this regard. Feeling as if even the British authorities had failed to see the true side of the scheme byt not recognizing the real value and function of the Sikh literary tradition, McLeod thought it proper to tell the London authorities that :[36]

> The main value which their literature must have for the European world results from its developing the spirit of the Sikh faith, which can be learned thoroughly from them, and into this spirit, or into the genious of Sikh race, it may perhaps be doubted whether Dr. Trumpp has everfully entered.

In India nothing was heard of the translation project between May 1872 and February 1873. On February 23, the Government of India asked the opinion of Govt. of Punjab about Trumpp's proposal that the Rahitnamas 'merit translation in preference to the book known as the Granth of the 10th Padshah'.

Accordingly, the Punjab administration asked the officiating Director Public Instruction to make an enquiry on the subject. The enquiry was conducted during the four months from March.[37] The enquiry officer consulted (I) the Anjuman/

35. Donald McLeod's Letter, *op. cit.*

36. Donald McLeod's Letter, *op. cit.*

37. For this development leading to enquiry see, *Progds. For-Gen., A,* Sep. 1873, nos. 6-10.

i/Punjab, (II) the choosen Granthis in Amritsar and Lahore, and (III) the individuals like Attar Singh Bhadour, Pandit Radhakishan and Bhai Budh Singh.

C. Pearson was the enquiry officer. His report made on June 30, 1873, disclosed that he had met Trumpp in Lahore and discussed with him 'the subject of the second Granth'.[38] Pearson did not mention the day or result of the meeting. He also did not state his status and purpose.

Pearson further revealed that he was impressed with the views expressed by Pandit Radhakishan and Bhai Budh Singh.[39] The enquiry officer recorded that he had consulted the Bhai on the advice of Donald McLeod. What was Budh Singh's relation with McLeod? or what was Radhakishan's relation with Pearson? It is not known.

Pandit Radhakishan told Pearson that the contemporary Sikhs 'disregarded the Rahitnamas', and they did not follow the scriptures either. According to the Pandit the Sikhs were guided entirely by an oral tradition and their scriptures "have no practical influence upon their manner of life."[40]

Pearson's report maintained that Bhai Budh Singh supported the main argument of the Pandit by saying that the people learn 'all the religion by word of mouth'. The Bhai considered the Rahitnamas 'were written by different persons about forty years after the death of Gobind Singh'.[41] At the start the people followed the rules contained therein "but the books and rules have now both gone out of fashion."[42]

Basing himself largely upon the views of the Pandit and the Bhai, Pearson observed that enquiry showed that "the Sikhs have invented sacred books rather in imitation of the scriptures of other religions than because the spirit of their

38. *Ibid.*, no. 6.

39. *Ibid.*

40. *Ibid.*, no. 7.

41. *Ibid.*

42. *Ibid.*

religion lived in written traditions."[43] However, Pearson did not reject the Sikh holy books or the Rahitnamas entirely. He suggested that "the portions of the Granths' and of the Rahitnamas deserved to be explained. It might help in presenting in a better way 'the history of Sikh religion'.[44]

But Pearson conceded that his views were not shared by others. In fact, there was two more and different views on the subject. First, the Granthis from Amritsar and Lahore together with Sardar Nihal Singh Chhachhi believed that 'of the two works (Rahitnamas and the Dassam Granth) the Granth is more important and should be preferentially translated...'

Secondly, Sardar Attar Singh of Bhadour "entirely concures in the views of Dr. Trumpp."[45]

The Punjab Govt. choose to act in the name of Sardar Attar Singh. It outrightly rejected the opinion of the Sikh Granthis. The Lieutenant-Governor recommended that 'the translation of the Rahitnamas have the preference, but that, if possible, those portions of the Granth of the 10th Padshah which relate to the precepts of the doctorine of the Sikh religion be translated also'.[46]

The Calcutta endorsed the Punjab recommendations which were in fact the suggestion made by Trumpp in April 1872. On September 15, 1873, Govt. of India recommended that the Rahitnamas and 'the books written by Govind Singh' were important and that Trumpp should be asked to translate them.[47]

What was Pearson's enquiry important for? Certainly not for its conclusion. In fact it did not conclude anything because it had only elaborated on what Trumpp had said about the Dassam Granth in April 1872. It was understandable because Pearson had guided Trumpp in this matter while he was in

43. *Ibid.*

44. *Ibid.*

45. *Ibid.*, no. 9.

46. *Ibid.*, no. 8.

47. *Ibid.*, no. 10.

Punjab. To what an extent Trumpp's negative attitude towards the Dassam Granth was influenced by Pearson's advice given before February 1872, it is yet to be seen. However, the fact remains that Pearson had a more clear and definite view of Sikh literature and tradition and he wanted the translation project to move along a particular way. In his June 1873 enquiry report he suggested that Trumpp should be asked to produce a 'history of Sikh religion' in the light of judiciously selected portions from the Adi Granth, the Dassam Granth (only the works of Guru Gobind Singh) and the Rahitnamas. It plainly meant that there was no need for the British and the translator to go for the complete translation of the Adi Granth, too. Unlike McLeod, Pearson wanted the translator, Trumpp, to be a historian of Sikhism based upon Bani and Rahit.

Pearson's enquiry certainly changed the mode and objective of the translation project by focussing upon the nature of contemporary Sikhism. It is again interesting to note that his suggestion of making a new history of Sikhism had already been adopted by Trumpp as shown by the latter's letter written in January 1873 to the London officials. What did this convergence of ideas between Trumpp and Pearson show? It showed only the kind of control the Lahore had exercised over the translator to give the project a locally desired goal.

In January 1873, Trumpp sent the first installment of his translation of the Adi Granth to London and promised to send more of it to make 500-600 pages in print in total.[48] He reported that his material would also include an INTRODUCTION, and the introductory part would comprise the 'life of Nanak from original Sikh sources'.[49] INTRODUCTION would also include the translators' remarks on the compositions in the Granth.

On the whole, Trumpp spoke very negatively about the language and theological and political value of the Book. He conceded his failure to find a new thing in the work. He did

48. See, *Trumpp's Letter dt. 13 January 1873 in Progds. For-Gen., A.* July 1873, nos. 34-37.

49. *Ibid.*

not see 'deism' or a combination of Hinduism and Islam in it.[50] The Adi Granth was, he said, full of "common Hindu Pantheism as set fourth in the Vedant and in the Bhagavat Gita."[51] Its devotional hymns were poor in conception, clumsy in style, and wearisome to read. The composition did not yield 'any doctorine' or a 'moral system' higher to 'the level of the common Hindu morality'.[52] In short, Trumpp denied an originality to both the language of the Granth and the thought of Guru Nanak. It was, asserted the translator, from Kabir that "Nanak and his successors have borrowed all they know and preach."[53]

Also, Trumpp sought to explain superficially what he was expected to show clearly and minutely by the administration. *Viz.,* the source of Sikh polity and its strength. He made a distinction between the ideas of the Gurus and their organizational contributions. His explanation reads :[54]

> In fact so much is clearly seen from the Granth itself, that the Sikh Gurus taught nothing new whatever and if a separate religious system and partly a new nationality has in course of time sprung up from it, this is not owing to the doctorines taught by them, but to their financial and political organization, which they gave to their disciples, and to the weakness of the Mughal Government.

The London sent Trumpp's translations to R. Rost, the Librarian of the India office, for his comments and suggestions. Rost made three recommendations. First, there was no need to translate and publish the whole Granth for it was teemed 'with repititions and trivialities'.[55] Instead, wrote he, 'an

50. *Ibid.*
51. *Ibid.*
52. *Ibid.*
53. *Ibid.*
54. *Ibid.*
55. *Ibid.,* no. 36.

abstract or selection of the most telling passages might suffice.'[56]

Secondly, Rost said that since the Adi Granth did not exhaust the Sikh writings so 'it stands to reason whether it may not be found desireable from political considerations to have a printed translation of the whole body of the sacred code of the Sikhs'.[57] The Librarian was highly appreciative of Trumpp's 'notes' that he saw as "a rich store-house of the most varied and original information on every subject connected with the history and creed of the Sikhs."[58] Thirdly, Trumpp's translation 'together with introduction and notes would cost £ 985-15 for 300 copies.[59]

The Secretary of state for India informed the Government of India that Rost did not favour the printing of the work 'from a purely literary point of view'.[60] The Calcutta was once again advised to enquire from the Punjab, its officers, native gentlemen, and the Granthis to state 'whether the political objects to be attained by the publication of the work are at all commensurate with the out-lay to be incurred....'[61] The Lahore was also to enquire and state if the political objects might not be obtained 'by the printing and publication of judiciously selected extracts of the work.'[62]

The drama of enquiry was again enacted in the Punjab.[63] The enquiry officer was again C. Pearson. He personally consulted Bhai Budh Singh, Bhai Pratap Singh, Rai Mul Singh, Pandit Radhakishan, Bhai Harbhagat Singh and Baba Khem Singh Bedi. Through the Deputy Commissioner of Amritsar

---

56. *Ibid.*

57. *Ibid.*

58. *Ibid.*

59. *Ibid.*

60. *Ibid.*

61. *Ibid.*

62. *Ibid.*

63. The enquiry details are found in *Progds. For-Gen.,* Jan. 1874, nos. 1-5.

were consulted the Gyanis like Gyan Singh, Tara Singh, Sant Singh, Santokh Singh, Nihal Singh and Pandit Saleg Ram. An other class consulted in Amritsar was that of 'educated and intelligent Sikh Gentlemen' like Sardar Thakur Singh Sandhawalia, Dyal Singh Majithia, Lehna Singh and Gurdit Singh.[64]

What did Pearson ask these gentlemen? What was his method of investigation? The clue to these issues was provided by the title of his final report that ran 'Notes of conversation held with a view to ascertain if the Adi Granth throws any light on the political history of the Sikhs'. The interviewees were put the following three set of questions directly or indirectly :[65]

1. What were the contents of the Adi Granth and the Rahitnamas? What were their status and function in the Sikh tradition?
2. What was the link between Sikhism and the Sikh Rule under Ranjit Singh? How did Sikh polity work?
3. Was there any difference between Sikhism and Hinduism? Who were the Kukas?

According to Pearson, Bhai Budh Singh, Bhai Pratap Singh and Rai Mul Singh denied that there was a link between Sikh scriptures and Sikh polity under Ranjit Singh. 'God only knows how the Sikh empire grew up. It had nothing to do with Sikh religion',[66] said Budh Singh, Pratap Singh asserted that pilgrimage and image worship were not the parts of Sikh creed. 'It is not right to follow the customs of the Hindus. Some Sikhs do, but owing to their ignorance and wickedness'[67], said Pratap Singh.

Rai Mul Singh felt embarrased over Pearson's query about the Hindu Sikh differences.[68] The Rai said Maharaja Ranjit

64. *Ibid.*, nos. 3, 5.

65. *Ibid.*

66. *Ibid.*, no. 3.

67. *Ibid.*

68. *Ibid.*

Singh treated the Brahmins 'honourably'.[69] Significantly, Pearson reported that Rai Mul Singh and many other Pandits 'considered Dr. Trumpp's translation all wrong'. They charged him of "giving his own meaning to passages and would not listen to the interpretation of the Bhais."[70]

But Pandit Radhakishan said that there was nothing like Sikh religion different from Hinduism. The Granth could't teach some thing new because Guru Nanak and Guru Gobind Singh were "but good Hindus."[71] As to the nature of Kuka movement, Pearson put the following in the mouth of Pandit :[72]

> The Kukas had invented a religion of their own which they said they got out of the Granths. They put aside the Hindu religion entirely, and had their own ceremonies for marriage and funerals... The idea of the Kukas was quite new. The Granths had nothing to do with it, and a translation could give no help to understand it.

In Pearson's report the Amritsar enquires showed that 'the political objective to be attained by the publication of the Adi Granth might be equally secured by the printing and publication of the extracts.'[73] Because there were 'very few portions of the Adi Granth which have any political bearing at all.'[74]

Pearson also reported that the Adi Granth was 'revered and worshipped almost as itself a divinity'. Unlike the Dassam Granth, the Adi Granth was found 'in every educated Sikh's house and most generally in Sikh Dharamsalas throughout the land'.[75] Dyal Singh Majithia said that while 'hundreds' of

69. *Ibid.*

70. *Ibid.*

71. *Ibid.*

72. *Ibid.*

73. *Ibid.*, no. 5.

74. *Ibid.*

75. *Ibid.*

the Adi Granth were found in private houses in Amritsar "there might not be ten copies of the Dassam Padshah Ka Granth."[76]

On the basis of these enquiries, the Punjab Government on December 9, 1873, recommended that the publication of the translation of the whole Adi Granth would be useless." The Punjab Secretary recorded, "I am to add that Sardar Attar Singh of Bhadour, who was likewise consulted, expressed his opinion that the whole Granth does not merit translation."[77]

Thus by the close of the year 1873, the original translation project to have the Adi Granth and Dassam Granth produced in English language for the European scholarship and the British administration came to an end. Its end was made in the name of 'educated Sikhs' by the provincial regime. It authorized Trumpp to compile what Pearson had named 'a history of Sikh religion' based upon selections from the Granths. The Adi Granth and the Rahitnamas were to be its more important sources. Griffin, Attar Singh, John Newton, Sardha Ram Philouri and Pearson were there to show him the way. The Janamsakhi and other Sakhis were available to him.[78] The British administrators and the missionaries had made him aware of the political and ideological issues before the contemporary Sikhism. His history of Sikhism was expected to help the cause of reformation of the Sikhs against the Kukas and Hindus.

The vaccum created by Trumpp's dissociation from Dassam Granth and the Rahitnamas was filled by Sardar Attar Singh Bhadour. At his own he came forward to translate the Rahitnamas and the works of Guru Gobind Singh.[79] The British search for, what Rost had called, 'the Sikh code' led them to informally engage the Sardar as an other translator.

To begin with Sardar Attar Singh was to make a Gurmukhi and Urdu abstract of the Dassam Granth portions and the

76. *Ibid.*

77. *Ibid.*, nos. 1-2.

78. See, Nazer Singh, *The Khalsa Towards Singh Sabha, op. cit.*

79. See, *Progds. For-Gen., A,* July, 1874, nos. 1-4.

two Rahitnamas. It was ready by March 1874. He requested the Calcutta to send the Gurmukhi version to Trumpp.[80] The Sau Sakhi had already been sent to the German Doctor (Trumpp).

The Urdu version was examined by E.C. Bayley who found that there was more than one version of the book. He agreed with Attar Singh in that it would be worthwhile to have the translation of the first (the Jap), the second (the Akal Ustat), the third (Vachittar Natak) and the fourteenth (Sandkian) and the first section of the sixteenth (Zaffarnama) chapters. "These are all that contain anything original"[81], reads Bayley's note.

Bayley suggested that the above mentioned portion of the Book could be compared to the Adi Granth to see the contrast between the ideas of unitarian 'Hindu reformers or Philosophers' of the Adi Granth and "the religion of the Dassam Padshah Ka Granth, the religion of the Sikhs as a political body."[82]

For Bayley, the Dassam Granth contained a great deal of fabled history and myth from 'the later hinduism'.[83] Also it had some portions translated from the Persian literature 'intended to inculcate merely wordly caution and prudence'.[84]

Further in Bayley's view the difference in the two Sikh Granths was a difference between two forms of the religion. The Adi Granth stood for the 'esoteric' while the Dassam Granth had the 'exoteric' form of religion. "The later for practical purpose is the more useful in a students point of view than the first"[85], wrote he.

Significantly, Bayley felt that the Rahitnamas of Nand and Prehlad were ideologically more akin to the Adi Granth than

80. *Ibid.*

81. See, *E.C. Bayley's Note in Progds. For-Gen., A,* July, 1874, nos. 1-4.

82. *Ibid.*

83. *Ibid.*

84. *Ibid.*

85. *Ibid.*

the Dassam Granth. His note reads "The Rahitnamas are really, it would seem, dependencies, so to speak, of the first work, and curious only as illustrative of it."[86]

On July 14, 1874, the abstract of Dassam Granth by Attar Singh was sent to England by the Government of India.[87] He was asked to translate the Jap, Akal Ustat, Bachittar Natak, the Sandkean and the first section of Zaffarnama into Urdu.

Attar Singh agreed to it but suggested that he would like to start with the Vachittar Natak[88] and Zaffarnama. His suggestion was accepted.

The Urdu translation of Zaffarnama and the Rahitnama reached Calcutta in October 1874. These were rendered into English by Captain Jarret and sent to England in January 1875.[89]

However, Attar Singh's translations also failed to satisfy the Calcutta authorities. Jarret found them meaningless and unintelligible. He said his own work of rendering them from Urdu into English was 'heart breaking'. In June 1875, the Punjab Secretary. T.H. Thompton, was instructed to throw the loyal Sikh translator 'a plight hint to hold his hand'.[90]

By September 1875, the London showed that it was no longer interested in the Sikh scriptures' translation. But the Sardar was persistant. In November, 1876, he sent his Urdu translation of the Jap, Akal Ustat, and the Sandkian to Calcutta. In this way Attar Singh completes the work undertaken by him'.[91]

---

86. *Ibid.*

87. *Ibid.*

88. See, *Progds. For-Gen., A,* Sep.1874, nos. 59-61.

89. See, *Progds. For-Gen., A,* March 1875, nos. 38-43.

90. See, *The Memo in Progds. For-Gen., A.* June 1875, nos. 21-24.

91. See, Punjab Govt's Letter no. 1848 dt. 22 Nov., 1876. *In Progds For-Gen., A,* Jan. 1877, nos. 16-17.

4 The Making of Sikh Scriptures—An Early Western View

This article deals with the book entitled *Sikhan de Raj de Vithia.* Its sole objective is to show the Historiographical nature of the work. The book deals with Sikh history, literature and Punjabi language. Moreover, it takes a definite view of the Sikh scriptures. Above all, the book had its own history. Its evolution starts in A.D. 1866 and continued through the 20th century. Between 1866 and 1956, it was translated from Punjabi into English more than once, it stood edited more than once. It's size and meaning varied with its editor/translator or commentator. This article is mainly based upon Henery Court's version of the *Vithia.*[1] But the works of Pritam Singh[2] and Gurbachan Kaur[3] have also been used.

A BRIEF OF THE *VITHIA*

The British administration in Punjab under Donald F. McLeod and the Ludhiana Mission of the American Presbyterians combined to produce a work on Sikh history in the Punjabi prose. Composed by Shardha Ram in 1866, and printed by Paderi Rudolph of, and at, the Ludhiana Mission Press in 1868, the work was entitled shortly as *Sikhan de Raj de Vithia.* Pandit Shardha Ram was the Munshi of John Newton and had worked with him. Newton and the Ludhiana press had trained him to produce 'the christian literature' in Urdu, Hindi and Punjabi.

In 1888, the *Vithia* was translated into English by Henery Court who enlarged it. Court also reported that Trumpp's

1. *History of the Sikhs;* OR, *Translation of the Sikhan de Raj de Vithia,* Henery Court (tr. and ed.). Language Deptt., Punjab, 1970.
2. Pritam Singh, *Sikhan de Raj de Vithia* (Pbi.), Jallundhar, 1956.
3. Gurbachan Kaur, *Shardha Ram Philouri* (Pbi.) (Patiala, 1988).

translation of and work on, the Adi Granth had been helpful to him in making the *Vithia* more communicative and meaningful.

The *Vithia* was partly translated into English for the second time in 1901 by Jawahar Singh. In 1901 it was entitled 'Selections From *Sikhan de Raj* de *Vithia*, with Notes'.[4]

Both Court and Jawahar Singh sought to amend Shardha Ram's work to make it more acceptable to the Sikhs. This evolution of *Sikhan de Raj de Vithia* from an 'un-sikh work' to more and more a 'Sikh work' makes the book an important piece of historical work.

The *Vithia* was edited by Pritam Singh in 1956. The editor showed some of the important additions and amendments made by Court.[5] With Pritam Singh, the *Vithia* again appeared in Punjabi. However, the editor excluded the Janam Sakhi portion. Gurbachan Kaur closely followed Pritam Singh.

THE ISSUE

The question of changing contents and language of the *Vithia* between 1866 and 1956 is very significant in its own way. Compare for a moment the title given to this work by the printers of 1868 with that of by Henery Court in 1888. The titles read :

1868	*1888*
Sikhan de Raj de *Vithia* Arthat Tinna de Dassan Guurian Ate Rajian da Jeuin, Birtanait Addik II Sahib Lokan de Prikhyia de Arath Sarkar de Aggia Nal Punjabi Bhakha Vich Banai Iss de Annat Vikhey Jannam Sakhi Vichon Bee Kai Katha Ghaddian Hann Ludhiana Paderi Rudolph	*History of the Sikhs; OR Translation of the Sikhan de Raj de Vithia.* AS LAID DOWN For the examination in Panjabi AND CONTAINING Narrative of the Ten Gurus, history of the Sikhs from the Rise of Maharaja Ranjit Singh to the occupation of the Punjab by

4. Jawahar Singh's work was published at Lahore in 1901.

5. See Pritam Singh, *op. cit.* pp. 18, 23, 24, 35, 39-40, 69-70.

Sahib de Jattan Nal Presybyterian Mission de Junttar Vich Chhapi 1868.	the English, a short Resume of the customs, rites, songs and proverbs of the Sikhs, and twenty discourses regarding events in the life of Guru Nanak, taken from the Janam Sakhi; or Life of Nanak. TOGETHER WITH A SHORT Gurmukhi Grammar AND An Appendix containing some useful technical words, in Roman characters.

But we leave it for the moment to fix our attention upon the concept of Scriptures in the Sikh tradition as recorded in Henery Court's version of the *Vithia*. Before seeing this concept, it will be useful to repeat that the book was consciously designed to be an educational and evangelical work. The Punjab Missionary Conference of Dec. 1862—January 1863 had advised various missions to be familiar themselves with the biographies of Guru Nanak and Guru Gobind Singh. Further the conference had exhibited a negative attitude towards the 10th Guru and the traditions associated with him. Hence a brief of the conference proceedings.

The missionaries and their associations in the region met on Dec. 31st 1862 and January 1st, 1863, at Lahore. It was the Ninth Session of the conference.[6] Both R.N. Cust and Donald F. McLeod participated. It were they who had mooted the idea of translation of Sikh Granths in 1857-1859. The conference deliberated upon a special essay written by Rev. William Keene of the Church Missionary Society, Amritsar. The essay was entitled 'The Sikhs : All that can be said about them, From a Missionary Point of View'.[7] Keene had been instructed to write

6. See, *Report of the Punjab Missionary Conference held at Lahore in December-January, 1862-63* (Lodiana : The American Presbyterian Mission Press, n.d). Keene's article will be referred as Keene's—Essay—N.S.

7. *Ibid.*, pp. 261-68.

on the Sikhs by the Committee of the conference. The essay was printed as a part of the Proceedings. In the proceedings Keene's essay was followed by an other piece of work entitled 'Vernacular Christian Literature : Suggestions for improving its character and Rendering it more Effectual, As a Means of Evangelisation to the Heathen, And of Edification to the Native Church'.[8] Rev. J. Newton took active part in the deliberations of the conference by opening discussion on the vernacular literature, the need to produce it and its function.

The conference was impressed with the Adi Granth. This book was found useful in preparing men to receive the word of Gospels.[9] It was noticed how Guru Nanak was interesting from the missionary point of view because of his emphasis upon the unity of God-head, and condemnation of popular Hinduism and its social practice such as caste, sati and idol-worship. Guru Nanak's freedom suited the missions[10] but not so its political transformation brought about by Guru Gobind Singh. In fact Keene felt that the transformation was nothing less than 'an evil'.[11]

The conference did not consider the ideas of Guru Gobind Singh. Logically there is only a passing reference to the Dassam Granth. Instead, it remembered William Carey for his Punjabi translation of the New Testament. Likewise the Ludhiana Mission was praised for making Grammar and Dictionary of Punjabi as well as the other thirty nine works produced by it in 'Sikh Colloquial'. It was informed that the Amritsar and Peshawar Missions were successful in converting 60 Sikhs to Christianity. Forty of the converts came from 'the 32nd Native infantary of the Mazhabi Sikhs'.[12] The missionaries dealing with the Sikhs were adviced to know the Vedant Philosophy and be "well acquainted with the biographies of Nanak and

8. *Ibid.*, pp. 268-86.

9. Keene's *Essay, op. cit.*, p. 265.

10. See, Keene's Essay, *op. cit.*, p. 262.

11. *Ibid.*, p. 265.

12. *Ibid.*, p. 266.

Govind".[13] Obviously, the Sakhi tradition was relevant. It's revival was certain.

Donald F. McLeod adviced the conference about the means by which evangelization could be secured more positively. He reminded that Punjab Govt.'s educational policy was designed by him in such a way that it could "lend its aid to those engaged in the preaching of the Scriptures".[14] The grant-in-aid system originated with him and it was a kind of help to the missions. Though the official policy of neutrality was to be followed yet the state officials could privately work for the missions, disclosed he.[15] After all, the Scriptures demands that every Christian be a member of 'Nation of priests'. Through Golaknath's the Raja of Kapurthala became a 'sypathizer' to Christianity. The Raja had met McLeod at Dharmsala[16], the conference was informed. Lastly, McLeod suggested that Heathenism could be attacked through the partial or separatist Hindus such as the Kabir Panthis, non-idolaters, tribes, and the deists.[17] The educated Indians too could be useful. The secular educationists had so far ignored the learning of the East. It was wrong, said McLeod. The learned classes were accessible "provided they are approached through the medium of their own learning".[18]

Significantly, Keene had told the conference how Guru Nanak's teachings in the Granth showed him as a separatist from the Hindus. The Guru's attitude towards idol-worship, sati and caste was different from the one held by the Hindus. Keene quoted Majh Ke War, Suhi and Asa Rag to substantiate his understanding of Sikhism on these issues.[19] The author also highlighted some other moral merits of the Bani that

13. *Ibid.,* p. 267.

14. *Ibid.,* p. 49.

15. *Ibid.,* pp. 110-11.

16. *Ibid.,* p. 126.

17. *Ibid.,* p. 132.

18. *Ibid.,* p. 154.

19. *Ibid.,* pp. 262-65.

declared 'murder, love of the world, covetousness and anger' as the four rivers of fire. Further, the Bani showed the futility of ceremonial abolutions, Keene was impressed by the Guru's word standing for forgiveness and redemption, and concluded :[20]

> The Granth aboundes in passage of this kind of which the greatest use could be made, in preaching the Gospels to the Sikhs.

THE SIKH SCRIPTURES AND THE *VITHIA*

A considerable portion of the *Vithia* is devoted to the lives of the ten Gurus. The origin and development of the Scriptures is related to lives and works of the Gurus. The fifth and the 10th Guru are more relevant. But out of all it is Guru Gobind Singh who has drawn a maximum space for himself in the *Vithia.* And the 10th Guru's treatment in this work begins with Guru's decision to create Khalsa.[21] Khalsa had it, a code at the hands of the Guru. The code included 'the Granth Sahib'.

How did *Sikhan de Raj de Vithia* present the lives of Sikh Gurus and their writtings, the Scriptures? Shardha Ram had a simple but wrong view of Guru in Sikhism. He denied unity to the ten Gurus. He designated Sri Chand as the Guru. The tenth Guru was different from Guru Nanak.[22] Guru Gobind Singh founded a new sect (the Khalsa) that was his own. Also, he had to have a Granth of his own (the Dassam Granth).[23] Before his death, the tenth Guru instructed his followers to follow 'the Granth Sahib'. In *de Vithia,* there is no reference to the guruship of Khalsa. Rather the work records that Khalsa worked without a leader for some time.[24] Hence, the question of Banda being Guru Gobind Singh's choice does't arise. The Guru's death in 1708 was so unbearable that many died after,

---

20. *Ibid.,* p. 265.
21. Henery Court, *op. cit.,* pp. 40-43.
22. *Sikhan de Raj de Vithia,* p. 54.
23. *Ibid.,* p. 43.
24. *Ibid.,* p. 60.

and for, him.[25] It was Naderr that decided the Sikh religious issues in case of controversy or difference.[26]

Shardha Ram was dead sure that the theoretical evolution of 'the Granth Sahib' was complete in 1604 A.D. itself. Because Guru Arjan Dev had closed its authorship against all Gurus to come save Guru Teg Bahadur.[27] Obviously, the ninth Guru had a limited chance as he was to fill merely the space left (actually allotted) for him in the Granth of 1604 A.D. Nevertheless, the verses of the 9th Guru were got written in Granth Sahib. Very logically the *Sikhan de Vithia* reminds how anything not written in the Granth Sahib was spurious for the Sikhs since the days of Guru Arjan.[28] Naturally, the Granth of 1604 A.D. was a bar against Guru Gobind Singh, implies *de Vithia*.

One day the tenth Guru 'took a fancy that he would send for the book of the Granth Sahib, and write something more in it'.[29] The book was with the Sodhis of Kartarpur who refused to give it to the Guru. The Sodhis entertained a doubt about the Guru's capacity to produce a new copy of the Granth. In face of this challenge, Guru Gobind Singh was silent but not for a long time. After a few days, he discovered that 'the original Granth Ji' was no longer suited his purpose because its reading was making the Sikhs 'very feeble hearted'.[30] So the Guru "determined himself to compose such a Granth, that, from reading it, his disciples, having learnt the science of government and the use of weapons, and other kinds of expertness, should become fit for fighting."[31] Thus the Dassam Granth was produced in 1753 B.K. *i.e.* 1696 A.D.[32]

---

25. *Ibid.*, p. 58.
26. *Ibid.*
27. *Ibid.*, p. 22.
28. *Ibid.*, p. 43.
29. *Ibid.*
30. *Ibid.*
31. *Ibid.*
32. *Ibid.*

The *Sikhan de Vithia* did not employ the name 'the Adi Granth' for the book began to be made since 1604 A.D. Instead, it called it as the Granth Sahib. More than once its author referred to the Dassam Granth also. The parts of Sastras were included in the Dassam Granth, he wrote. Guru Gobind Singh's 'religion was not confined to any one book or prophet or incarnation',[33] reads *de Vithia*. Yet it was upon the Granth Sahib that the tenth Guru confered Guruship before breathing the last, concluded Shardha Ram. Interestingly, the *Sikhan-de Raj de Vithia* refers to Damdama Sahib but not the Damdami Bir.[34]

The *Vithia* spoke minimum about Khalsa. It did not describe the great event that had happened in Anandpur on the Baisakhi of 1699 as the creation or foundation of Khalsa. Even the phrase 'Wah Guru Ji Ka Khalsa' had been translated as 'Say, O, Sect of the Wah Guru'.[35] Though it maintains that Guru Gobind Singh gave a written code to his disciples yet its concept of Rahit is totally deviod of the merits of Khalsa. 'The code of the Sikhs' given in the *Vithia* is brief, and all the attributes of a Sikh had been in the negative terms.[36] The only exception is the notion that the Granth Ji 'decrees'. For example the code says that if the Sikhs were to observe the Saradh or the Karam Kiria at all, they could "do so according to the decrees of the Granthji."[37] Similarly, the Sikhs could follow 'the Sastras' or 'the customs of the country" only "according to the decrees of the Granthji."[38]

The tenth Guru, says the *Vithia,* breathed his last while fully armed but having the CHOPAI (the Quatrain) on his lips.[39] The Quatrain's opening lines as translated by Trumpp

33. *Ibid.,* p. 54.
34. *Ibid.,* p. 46.
35. *Ibid.,* p. 41.
36. See, *Ibid.,* pp. 41-42.
37. *Ibid.,* p. 43.
38. *Ibid.*
39. *Ibid.,* p. 57.

had been given by Henery Court.[40] Interestingly, Trumpp for this portion had relied upon the original *Sikhan de Raj de Vithia* while its translator, Henery Court, choose to rely upon Trumpp.[41] Strangely Trumpp was wrong in quoting the originals as well in their translation.

There is strong echo of the Missionary Conference of 1862-63 in *Sikhan de Raj de Vithia.* It is evident from *(a)* its preference of Guru Nanak and the Adi Granth over Guru Gobind Singh and the Dassam Granth, *(b)* its conception of Guru Gobind Singh as a necessary 'evil'. The military and political aspect of his ideas and organization are referred without appreciation. Often they stand condemned, Khalsa and its Rahit are seldom taken positively, *(c)* the correspondence between the views of Guru Nanak and Guru Gobind Singh is noticed in those areas alone where Sikhism and Hinduism stood apart from each other, and *(d)* Granthji gets an added significance. Its message presents Guru Nanak and his movement in a new light. The Guru's views on unity of Godhood, the futility of many a rituals and social practices such as the sati and caste are shown relevant. The 'natural religion' of Guru Nanak frees the mind from many errors of gross Hinduism, reads the conference proceedings (p. 262) The *Vithia* says Guru Nanak's 'belief was some what different from the old Shastras, and books'. (p. 10). Guru Gobind Singh used the Sastra but not at the cost of Granthji, implies the Vithia. The Christian literature should be created but not at the total cost of Sikh Scriptures, cautioned the Missionary Conference.

40. See, *Ibid.,* Also Ernest Trumpp, *The Adi Granth* (Munshiram Manoharlal, 1997), xcv.

41. *Ibid.*

5 From Trumpp to Macauliffe

As a translator of the Sikh Scriptures Ernest Trumpp left a significant legacy for M.A. Macauliffe. First, Trumpp's translation project (1869-1877) had settled the issue of the definition of Sikh scripture by taking the Adi Granth in the Damdama Bir as the Guru Granth Sahib. Macauliffe need not, and he did not bother much about the Dassam Granth. Secondly, Trumpp had given importance to Janam Sakhi and Rahitnama literature along with some of the compositions in the Dassam Granth taken to be as the writings of Guru Gobind Singh.[1] In this also Trumpp was followed by Macauliffe. Thirdly, Trumpp had begun as a translator of the Adi Granth but did not complete it. Virtually, he turned out to be one more historian of the Sikhs. The same happened with Macauliffe, he also translated the Guru Granth partially. Lastly, Trumpp had recognized the need to develop Punjabi language, Macauliffe advocated the cause of Punjabi as a vehicle of preserving Sikhism.[2]

Yet the difference between Trumpp and Macauliffe was great. Trumpp's was an official undertaking. Enterprize of Macauliffe was voluntary being originated with him and the Sikh community. Further, Trumpp had been associated with a particular Church while Macauliffe was a civil servant of a state supposed to be secular. Secondly, the method and

1. See, E. Trumpp, *The Adi Granth* (Munshiram Mohanlal, 1977), XCI, note 5.

2. See, N.G. Barrier, 'Trumpp and Macauliffe', in, Fauja Singh (ed.), *Historians and Historiography of the Sikhs* (New Delhi, 1978), pp. 166-85. Also W.H. McLeod, *Guru Nanak and the Sikh Religion* (Oxford, 1968).

approach of Trumpp was vastly different from the one followed by Macauliffe. The former was a peddler trying to cover a very vast field. The latter had Sikh individuals, organizations and committees to help and correct him. Trumpp failed to shed his negative bias against the given Sikh wisdom in the Guru Granth, and continued to underplay, ignore and discard the knowledge of Gyanies and Granthis.[3] Unlike him, Macauliffe choose to rely upon the traditional interpretors of Sikhism. Advisors such as C. Pearson, Attar Singh Bhadour and L.H. Griffin in Punjab were available to Trumpp, nay, were ready to help him but he declined to avail their services. No such inhibition was displayed by Macauliffe who mobilized many more Indians and Europeans to join him.[4]

Thirdly, Trumpp had no interest in his work for various reasons such as the sheer volume of the work, his own poor health and his inability to see clearly the purpose of the task given to him. It was not Sikhism or the issues before the British Empire *i.e.* the political condition or potential of the Sikhs that had motivated Trumpp. The only motivation for Trumpp was the historical linguistics or philology.[5] Macauliffe's position was different. He was an 'insider' who had lived with the Sikhs and dealt with the Empire. He was fully aware about the issues before the contemporary Sikhs. It was his public spirit that had led him to work on the translation, and it was he who was to determine its course and goal. Moreover, he knew as to for whom he was writing and why.[6] Macauliffe

3. N.G. Barrier, *op. cit.*, p. 168.
4. See, Macauliffe's article 'The Holy Writings of the Sikhs' in, Darshan Singh (ed.), *Western Image of the Sikh Religion* (New Delhi, 1999), pp. 316-23. The article first appeared in three parts through the Asiatic Quarterly Review, April-Oct., 1898.
5. See, our Appendix, no. 05.
6. Macauliffe had to refer to his position and the purpose of his work again and again because he was seeking Government's patronage even since 1892. The patronage was denied to him in a very subtle and long way. The whole exercise lasted upto 1910. Between 1892 and 1910, Macauliffe submitted his case to the Administration many

(Contd.)

had a mission because he was a committed translator. He was committed to *(a)* establish that Sikhism was different from all other religions including Hinduism, and *(b)* help in bridging the gap between the British and the English educated Sikhs so that a positive political relationship between the Empire and the Sikh community could be consolidated.[7]

While dealing with the mission of Macauliffe, it will be useful to keep in mind that his mission took its shape gradually. His association with the British Punjab began in 1864 but it was only by 1880 that he became interested in the Sikhs. Further, his early articles on the Sikhs (1880-01)[8] were related to the historical development of Sikhism rather than the Sikh Scriptures as such. In fact, it was in February 1890 that he was reported as the one doing the translation of 'the sacred book of the Sikhs'. Recently, McLeod and Barrier have suggested that Macauliffe's articles of 1880-81 had a different approach and conclusions than that of in his writings after 1893.[9] We know that in this year (1893) he resigned from the British civil service to work on the translation of Guru Granth.

The philosophical and methodological difference between the early Sikh and the later Sikh writing of Macauliffe underlines only his changing relationships with the Sikh leadership in the first instance. Secondly it indicates the

---

(Contd.)

a time, and each time he sought to clarify the nature and objectives of his undertaking. His correspondence with the Government can be seen in *Proceedings Home-public, B,* January 1900, nos. 125-128 *(N.A.I.), Progds. Home Public,* June, 1898 no. 183, and *Progds.* Home B and P, A, June 1907, nos. 121-22 (N.A.I.).

7. See, Macauliffe's letter dated 9 Dec., 1899, to Lawrence, Secretary to Viceroy, in *Proceedings, Home-Public, B,* January 1900, nos. 125-28 (N.A.I.).

8. The articles were *(i)* 'The Diwali at Amritsar : The Religion of the Sikhs', *(ii)* 'The Rise of Amritsar and the Alterations of the Sikh Religion' and *(iii)* 'The Sikh Religion under Banda and its Present condition'. For these see, Darshan Singh, *op. cit.,* pp. 229-84.

9. See, N.G. Barrier, *op. cit.,* W.H. McLeod, ᵇmax Arthur Macauliffe, *in Exploring Sikhism* (Oxford, 2000), p. 260.

transformation that the Singh Sabha was passing through. On both these accounts the difference is significant. But it needs to be noticed that even in 1880-81, Macauliffe was in touch with the enlightened Sikh individuals and he respected their opinion. For the article 'The Rise of Amritsar and the Alterations of the Sikh Religion', he was indebted to Sardar Dyal Singh, 'a Sikh gentleman, who has visited England and made himself acquanted with our literature and customs'.[10] His next article 'The Sikh Religion under Banda and its Present Condition' acknowledged that it was partly based upon Rattan Singh Bhangu's *Panth Prakash* as supplied in the manuscript form to Macauliffe by Attar Singh Bhadour. This article concedes that it was also based upon 'an urdu paper' prepared by 'one of the chief priests of the temple'.[11] Macauliffe's treatment of the Akalis in this article was influenced by the urdu paper especially made for him.

One more continuity from Macauliffe's so-called early writings to later writings may be noticed. 'The Diwali at Amritsar : the Religion of the Sikhs' ended by refering to the difference between 'the early religion of the Sikhs' and the one as actually found by Macauliffe. The article promised that the 'alterations and corruptions of the Sikh religion would subsequently be described'.[12] The promise was kept through 'The Sikh Religion under Banda'. More significantly, it was the later article that identified Hinduism and its strength and vitality or 'the boa constrictor' like quality as to be chief source of danger to Sikhism.[13] This argument first advanced by G.W. Leitner[14] became a profound theoretical premise with

---

10. See, Macauliffe, 'The Rise of Amritsar', in Darshan Singh, *op. cit.*, p. 363, note 08.
11. See, Macauliffe, 'The Sikh Religion under Banda', in Darshan Singh, pp. 228, 280.
12. See, Macauliffe, 'The Diwali at Amritsar', in Darshan Singh, *op. cit.*, p. 239.
13. See, Macauliffe, *op. cit.*, p. 283.
14. See, Nazer Singh, *Delhi and Punjab : Essays in History and Historiography* (New Delhi, 1995), p. 67.

Macauliffe who expressed it constantly. So did the Singh Sabha, first, the Lahore Sabha and by 1898 the Amritsar Sabha, too. It will be useful to note that Macauliffe was, like Leitner, associated with the Singh Sabha.

The most significant discontinuity in Macauliffe's early and later writings was his attitude towards Trumpp and his work. In 'the Diwali at Amritsar' Macauliffe acknowledged his debt "to the work of this laborious German for facilitating my study of the religion of the early Sikh Apostels."[15] However, Macauliffe in 'The Holy writings of the Sikhs' found a number of drawbacks in Trumpp's translation. The drawbacks were *(i)* the translator was a German (ex) missionary, *(ii)* out of 31 ragas only four were translated, *(iii)* he could't write English correctly, *(iv)* the traditional interpretations were ignored (v) the theological zeal of Trumpp led him to remark upon the doctrines of Sikhism and on the Gurus.[16]

The clue to Macauliffe's changing attitude towards Trumpp and his translation could be found in his new relationship with the Sikhs by 1892. On February 25, 1892, he told the Punjab authorities that Trumpp's translation might be of some help to "the English students of the Sikh religion, but I am obliged to join the Sikhs in their unanimous condemnation of the translation."[17] It was before he left for Europe on furlough. He further said that he desired to 'put his researches into the religion of the Sikhs into some tangible form' before his departure to Europe. Moreover, he said that the translation of the whole Granth would not be possible. Macauliffe further disclosed that he had already collected material on the lives of the Bhagts from Alwar, Jaipur and Benaras and in this work he had been helped by Gyani Tara Singh of Patiala. Obviously, Macauliffe in Ferozepur was looking for an opportunity. It is evident from the fact that in his Feb. 25, 1892 letter he expected his research to be of some use to the Patiala chief who was getting the Guru Granth translated into Punjabi.

15. Macauliffe, *op. cit.,* p. 245, note 48.

16. See, Macauliffe, *op. cit.,* pp. 316-18.

17. See, Macauliffe's letter dt. 25 Feb. 1892 Quoted in *Progds. Home-Public,* June 1898 no 183 (N.A.I.).

Between 'the Diwali at Amritsar' (April, 1880) and 'the Holy Writings' (1898) Macauliffe's relationship with the Singh Sabha had changed. Moreover, the Singh Sabha movement itself had changed considerably. The year 1884 witnessed the emergence of Singh Sabha as an important educational movement in Punjab.[18] The Lahore Singh Sabha celebrated its sixth anniversary on 31st January 1885. G.W. Leitner and Macauliffe addressed the Sabha on the very first day.[19] According to *the Tribune,* Macauliffe remarked that 'there is not a single Sikh in the Punjab who can effectively explain the Granth'.[20] Upon it the paper commented that Macauliffe's remark "reflects discredit on the Sikhs", and hoped that the Sabha "will take lesson from this passing remark and set-out about working out measures where this stigma will be blotted off from their heads."[21] In April, 1885, the Lahore Khalsa Diwan, mooted the setting up of Khalsa College.

Going by the Tribune's report, Macauliffe was working on the Sikh Scriptures at his own. In fact, he himself tells that ever since he wrote his article 'The Diwali at Amritsar' he had been fascinated by the Scriptures. He had also employed a granthi to help him in understanding them.[22]

We know that criticism of Trumpp, his method and findings were a matter of opinion ever since 1871. His first critics were Donald F. McLeod and R.N. Cust. The British enquiry made in 1873 had also shown that the Pandits in Lahore had disapproved Trumpp's method. However, the organized and negative Sikh reaction against him came in November, 1888 when an Address to this effect was made to Governor-General Lord Duffrin.[23] The Address reminded the Government that Trumpp's translation was officially

18. *The Tribune,* Lahore, Feb. 7, 1885 (Editorial).

19. *Ibid.,* Feb. 7, 14, 1885.

20. *Ibid.,* Feb. 7, 14, 1885.

21. *The Tribune,* Lahore, 18 April, 1885.

22. See, Macauliffe, 'The Holi Writings', *op. cit.,* p. 316.

23. *Ibid.*

undertaken, and it was a 'useless labour' and 'money spent in vain' because its language was 'wide of the meaning'. Macauliffe quoted the Sikh Address of 1888 in his third article on 'The Holy writings of the Sikhs' published in *the Asiatic Quarterly Review,* Oct. 1898.

In February, 1890, *the Echo* reported that a "new English translation of the sacred book of the Sikhs is now being written by Mr. Macauliffe, of the Bengal Civil Service".[24]

Macauliffe was posted as the Divisional Judge, Ferozepur, in early 1892. In Feb. 1892, he sought Government's permission to go on leave partly to complete and publish his work on the Sikhs. On March 14, the Punjab Govt. informed him that his request could not be granted.[25] In protest, he went on a Furlough to Europe. The Furlough was to end in May, 1893.[26] On May 4, 1893, Secretary of the Lahore Khalsa Diwan, Gurmukh Singh, wrote to Macauliffe that the Ferozepur Singh Sabha wanted him to act as the translator of Guru Granth. The Sabha and the Diwan advised him to move his Govt. to get himself appointed 'on special duty like Dr. Trumpp to complete the translation'. He and the Govt. were free to adopt any other course too. Letter of the Diwan said that the request was 'an index of the opinion of the educated Sikh community'. The Diwan was sure that Macauliffe would do the needful for he had already with him a considerable portion of the Granth translated.

Macauliffe had a personal meeting with the Secretary of the Diwan. The latter assured him that the Diwan would work for him "in the same manner as it had undertaken the Khalsa College project."[27] Macauliffe was further assured that he would be fully compensated "for the losses he had suffered

---

24. See, Macauliffe quoted in *Progds. Home-Public* B, January, 1900, nos. 125-28 (N.A.I.).

25. See, Punjab Government's Letter dt. 12 May, 1898, in *Progds. Home-Public,* June, 1898, no. 183 (N.A.I.).

26. Macauliffe Quoted in *Progds. Home-Public,* 13, June 1900, *op. cit.*

27. *Ibid.*

by the failure of Joint Stock Companies."[28] He was made to believe that Govt's 'aid' and sanction would be secured 'within one or two months'.

Macauliffe agreed to resign his post and actually resigned it. Between 1893 and December, 1897, he worked on the translation, "the task the Sikhs assigned me".[29] For about three years he worked in Amritsar. Both in 1896 and 1897 he in vain tried to seek Punjab Government's patronage for work. Between January 1897 and March 1898, he thrice wrote to the Chief Secretary, Punjab, for this purpose. Each time he assured that he would not produce any thing not acceptable to the Sikhs. He frankly admitted that no help would come his way unless the Government took the lead in this direction.[30] Macauliffe narrated how the chiefs of Patiala and Nabha had turned their back to his scheme. Gurmukh Singh had backed out and turned to be an opponent to him. In March, 1898 the chief of Nabha did not permit Kahn Singh to join him. Also, Sunder Singh Majithia and the Amritsar Singh Sabha were denied the services of Sardar Sadhu Singh, a forest officer of Chamba State to assist a Sikh committee to examine the new translation.[31]

In December 1897, Macauliffe issued a circular letter to the Sikhs. He informed that (1) he had incured a debt of Rs. 35,000 on account of his researches, (2) spent his considerable time in the old age, and (3) the work was 'volumnious' as he wanted to supplement his translation with the life sketch of Guru Gobind Singh and the other Bhagats.[32]

In the mean time he had attended the Congress of the Orientalists held in Paris. He had presented his paper 'The Holy Writings of the Sikhs' before the Congress. The paper

---

28. *Ibid.*
29. Macauliffe, 'The Holy Sikh Writings, *op. cit.,* p. 317.
30. Macauliffe's Letter to Lawrence, *op. cit.*
31. The Punjab Chief Secretary, Dane's letter to Sunder Singh Majithia, dt. 5 March, 1898, Quoted in *Progds. Home-Public,* June 1898, no. 183 (N.A.I.).
32. Macauliffe, Quoted in *Progds. Home, Pub,* 13, Jan, 1900, *op. cit.*

was published by the *Asiatic Quarterly Review* for April, July and October, 1898. Through the paper's last installement, Macauliffe described the origin, motives, circumstances and the state of his undertaking.[33] Macauliffe's brief of past and present of his undertaking had the following three basic features :

(i) A considerable emphasis was laid down upon the incorrectness of Trumpp's translation and the Sikh objection to it. Macauliffe fully shared the Sikh view that the total result of the translation "is rather deterimental than advantageous to the religion of the Sikhs".[34]

(ii) Another translation was "necessary in all interests".[35] In Europe, America, Australia and even in India itself, Macauliffe was confronted with the question "what the Sikh religion was, and whether the Sikhs were Hindus, idolators, or Muhammadans; and I thought it was not good even for the Sikhs themselves that this ignorance regarding their religion should be allowed to continue."[36] He hoped that his translation would introduce the Sikhs to the worled properly and doing so it would be of "political advantage to them."[37]

Elsewhere but at the same time Macauliffe had told the Government that the Sikhs were 'mortally offended at the work of a previous translator. If they had been still loyal to the British it was for they hate the Muslims "who did to death three of their Gurus; and if a Christian Government insults their religion, and will make them no reparation, the consequences may be more serious than expected."[38]

*(iii)*Macauliffe expanded his list of the advantages likely

33. See, Darshan Singh, *op. cit.,* 316-323.

34. *Ibid.*, p. 317.

35. *Ibid.*

36. *Ibid.*

37. *Ibid.*

38. Macauliffe Quoted in *Progds. Home-Public 13,* Jan, 1900, *op. cit.*

to flow from his work. First, it would preserve the traditional Sikh knowledge, more so the wisdom of the gyanies. *(ii)* the translation would help fixing the meaning of words in the Granth that were becoming obsolete. His translation might lead to its translations into Punjabi and Hindi. All this would make the message of the Granth accessible to the masses. *(iii)* The high ethical principles of Sikhism would be beneficial to the whole world. *(iv)* the knowledge of Sikh tradition was an acknowledged administrative practice and need of the British.[39]

Macauliffe recorded that his scheme since 1892 had the support of Singh Sabha movement. Already he had addressed the Sikhs from the Akal Takhat.[40] Both the Darbar Sahib, Amritsar and the Amritsar Singh Sabha stood by him. We know that in Feb. 1898 an Akhand Path was performed for Macauliffe's success, and a committee of the Sikhs was constituted by the Sikh gathering at the Akal Takhat. The committee was to see and certify the correctness of the translation. The committee approved the translation and appealed to the Sikh Chiefs and Sardars to help Macauliffe.[41]

Incouraged by this as well as by the international appreciation of his work at the Rome Congress of the Orientalists in 1899, Macauliffe decided to approach Govt. of India. It was also because he had failed to convince the Punjab authorities (1892-1898). He had realized that the Government's approval was essential to induce the Sikhs "to adhere to their promise to me, and that my work may be published."[42]

The frankness and boldness with which Macauliffe had narrated publically the issues involved in his undertaking by 1898 showed only his helpness caused by the refusal of Punjab Govt. to patronize him. On April 27, 1898, the Punjab Secretary had informed him about his Government's negative reply in

39. 'The Holy Writings of the Sikhs', *op. cit.*, pp. 319, 323.

40. *Ibid.*, p. 321.

41. *Ibid.*, pp. 321-22.

42. *Ibid.*, p. 322.

this regard. The Secretary had found Macauliffe responsible for the situation in which he had landed himself.[43] Because the new translator had conceived the whole scheme in a wrong way. The Secretary said that there could be no comparision between the translation scheme under Trumpp and the one pursued by Macauliffe. The former was undertaken in the interest of 'Science'. Different was the case with Macauliffe. How could the Govt. supposed to be neutral in religious matters work for a particular religion or a religion of particular section? Indirectly, the Punjab administration saw Macauliffe's moves as a source of controversy centred on Trumpp's translation but directed against the Government as well.

For the time being Macauliffe was on the defensive. He needed money to get himself published. It was not forthcoming either from the Sikhs or the Government. He had identified himself completely with the Tat Khalsa. The Tat Khalsa elements were eagerly looking towards him and his translation.[44] The Singh Sabha movement had come to an end because a whole new Sikh leadership had emerged by 1899. Centred at Amritsar, the neo-Sikhs were religiously radical in the sense that they believed in the separate indentity of the Sikhs. Bound together by the ties of commerce, the Tat Khalsa or the neo-Sikhs yet looked towards the Government for their politics. The Curzon regime (1898-1905) was either indifferent to or suspect of the entire new development in Sikh life.

During 1899, Curzon visited both Lahore and Amritsar.[45] Both the Lahore Khalsa Diwan and the Amritsar Singh Sabha submitted memorials to him. The Lahore memorial asked the

---

43. Letter of Pb. Secy. to Macauliffe dt. 27 April 1898, *Progds. Home Pub.* June, 1898, *op. cit.*

44. A Pro Tat Khalsa newspaper, *The Khalsa* wrote on 8 March 1899, that with Macauliffe's translation new Sikh leadership of the English educated would emerge. The Sikh ideas would achieve clarity of meaning and the "Tat (pure) Khalsa will begin to start a new career."

45. 'The Sikh Address to the Viceroy' Quoted in *Progds. Home-Public, B,* Jan., 1900, op. cit.

Governor-General to get prepaired "a correct translation of our sacred scriptures made into English which will be worthy of our religion and our race, and which will remove the stigma Dr. Trumpp sought to attach to us for ever."[46] In reply, Curzon merely advised the Sikhs to undertake the task of translation themselves.[47]

The Amritsar memorial to Curzon was more comprehensive both in terms of Trumpp's criticism and the political relevance of a new translation. Referring to the political potentional of Macauliffe's exercize indirectly, the memorial reads :[48]

> Owing to the spread of English education under our benign Government, the rising generation are growing up in great ignorance of their sacred writings, and are either relapsing into Hinduism or are becoming indifferent to all religion, a result which we submit cannot be for the advantage of the State. If a trustworthy translation of our sacred writings were made for their use, they would remain true Sikhs and loyal as before to the British Government.

Curzon's advice to the Lahore Memorialists that they should do the translation themselves was repeated in reply to the Amritsar memorial. Not only this, Curzon's indifference was practized by the Secretary of State for India also. The State Secretary had been approached by Macauliffe through a representative of the Rome Congress of the Orientalists.[49]

By 1899 Macauliffe was practically in collusion with the British administration. He knew that the Amritsar Memorial was against 'the apathy' shown by the Punjab Government towards his scheme. The criticism of Trumpp was embarrasing to the British regime while the talk of 'advantage to state' or

---

46. *Ibid.*
47. *Ibid.*
48. 'Memorial of the Singh Sabha Amritsar', Quoted in *Progds., op. cit.*
49. See, M.A. Macauliffe, 'The Holy Scriptures of the Sikhs', in Darshan Singh, *op. cit.*, p. 382.

of 'the political advantage to the Sikhs' had politicized the whole issue like anything.

In May 1898 Macauliffe had submitted a Memorandum to the Govt. of India through the Punjab authorities. He had asked for a grant of Rs. 10,000 to publish his work. The Punjab did not send his memorandum. Nothing was heard of it till early 1902 when the Secretary of State intervened in the matter. In May, 1902, the Punjab administration headed by Charles Riwaz suggested that Macauliffe should be given Rs. 5,000 on two conditions.[50] First, he would raise Rs. 25,000 himself through the subscriptions. In this way he could meet his publication expenditure estimated to be Rs. 30,000 in all. Second, he would supply ten copies of his published work to the Government for use. Subsequently, the first condition was dropped on the ground that it might encourage the Punjab Chiefs to help the translation scheme because they might take it as a hint that the Government had approved it.[51] Also, the Govt. of India in April 1903 raised the demand of copies from ten to forty.

Again nothing was heard about the issue from April 1903 to June 1905.[52] Between June 1905 and January 1907, the Govt. of India made three enquiries in the matter from the Punjab administration. In 1905, it was told that Macauliffe had not drawn the money. In Oct, 1906, it was informed that the translator was not sure about the publication of his work. Macauliffe was not clear if the work was to be published in English or Punjabi.[53]

In January 1907, Macauliffe requested the Punjab Govt. to forward his memorandum of 25th May 1898 to Govt. of India that was lying with the former. The Punjab Government outrightly rejected his request.[54]

---

50. See, *Progds. Home-Public, A,* Feb. 1903, nos. 400-401 (N.A.I.).
51. Letter of the Secretary of State to Viceroy of India, at 24 Oct. 1902, in *Progds., Ibid.*
52. See, *Progds. Home-Public, A,* Feb, 1907, nos. 99-102 (N.A.I.).
53. *Ibid.*
54. *Ibid.*

Macauliffe's request was a signal for the renewal of the fight he and his Sikh supporters had been engaged in since 1897. The fight had assumed a new proportion. In early 1907 Tikka Parduman Singh of Nabha gave the notice of asking the following question in the Council of the Governor-General to be met on 1st March 1907.[55]

> 'will the Govt. be pleased to make reparation, and if so, of what nature, to the Sikhs for the insults offered to their Gurus, their sacred books, and their religion by a German Missionary appointed by the India office in 1869 to make a translation of Sri Guru Granth Sahib, or Bible of the Sikhs'.

The question was disallowed on the ground that it was not in public interest.[56] However, the Govt. noticed that the question was raised on Macauliffe's behest. It was either 'drafted or inspired' by him. The Govt.'s decision was conved to the Tikka on 27 Feb. 1907.[57]

However, on Feb. 5th 1907, Macauliffe made new memorandum to the Government. It was sent by the Punjab to Govt. of India on March 6, 1907.[58]

Again Macauliffe tried to clear the doubts about the nature and motives of his work. He wrote :[59]

> I intended my translation partly as a literary effort, and partly as a reparation to the Sikhs for the ridicule and insults cast on their religion by the German translator.

Stressing the literary aspect of his work this time with a greater vigour, Macauliffe maintained :[60]

---

55. See, *Progds. Home-Public, A,* March, 1907, no. 23 (N.A.I.).
56. *Ibid.*
57. *Ibid.*
58. See, Macauliffe's Memorial to Punjab Government dt. 5 Feb. 1907, in, *Progds., Home B and P, A,* June, 1907, nos. 121-22 (N.A.I.).
59. Macauliffe's Memorial, *op. cit.*
60. *Ibid.*

> My work in its present form need not be regarded as a religious one at all, nor is it a peculiarly Sikh work.

It was, continued he, a translation of 'ancient Indian compositions'.[61] The Granth contained the works of many Bhagats and in many languages.

The preservation of Sikhism against Hinduism and for the British empire could be secured only by a new and current translation available to the English educated Sikhs.[62] The Sikh Chiefs and the Sardars were yet to be involved in this huge task, wrote he.

Macauliffe closed his memorandum with a personal religious note. It reads :[63]

> Indeed Guru Arjan... left an injunction that it [Granth] should be translated into languages of foreigners, so that its teachings might spread over the whole world as the oil spreads over water. I am merely acting according to his instructions.

This time the Government was not so hostile to Macauliffe's move. It consided even to raise the demand from Rupees 10,000 into Rs. 15,000.[64] Yet it sanctioned nothing immediately. As if to delay the matter, Govt. of India asked the Punjab Government to make an assessment of the Sikh opinion in this regard. What was the guarantee that the translation would be completed?, it further asked.

On 6th May, 1908, the Govt. of India was informed by the Punjab that Macauliffe had given his material for publication to the Clarendon Press, Oxford.[65] He did not need any grant but would welcome a personal honrarium. Its amount might be £ 500.

As to the Sikhs, their educated portion, particularly 'the

---

61. *Ibid.*
62. *Ibid.*
63. *Ibid.*
64. See, Riseley's Note Macauliffe's Memorial in *Progds., op. cit.*
65. See, *Progds. Home B and P.* Sep. 1908, nos. 35-38.

Neo-Sikh school of thought', would find the translation useful for itself. In fact, the translation had been made 'from their point of view'. It would be popular with them. Further, Kahn Singh of Nabha was with Macauliffe to guide the translator and the printers. The Nabha Chief had sent him at the state expense. Moreover, the publication was not the translation of the scriptures as such but "a history of the Sikh Gurus and other Saints, and about them there can be hardly any controversy",[66] said the Punjab Govt.

On May 6, 1908, the matter was again referred to the Secretary of State for India.

On December 23, 1908, Macauliffe told H.S. Stuart that his INTRODUCTION and PREFACE were read by A.C. Lyall.[67] While the Preface stood approved by him, some 'omission' from the introduction were made. Some 'alterations' were made on the suggestion of Professor A.A. Macdowell, Boden Professor of Sanskrit at University of Oxford.

Macauliffe's letter of 26 Feb. 1909 to H.S. Stuart informed that his work would come out in April, 1909.[68] He requested him to send 'assistance' and assured that the help would not be disclosed through the Preface.

As the Government was not ready to give Macauliffe anything more than Rs. 5000 in all, so he refused to accept it finally.[69]

66. *Ibid.*

67. Macauliffe to Stuart dt. 23 Dec. 1898, in *Progds. Home B and P, A,* June, 1909, nos. 43-47.

68. *Ibid.*

69. *Ibid.*

6 Understanding the Sikhs Through Bani—Some Early Western Ways

Reason for writing this paper is simple. History had been an important way of knowing the Sikhs since the late 18th century. The Sikh Studies were European-nay-British by their conception and their motivation.[1] In this sense these were Western by their origin. The Sikh Studies recognized the significance of the Sikh scriptures as a more direct and authentic source of knowledge about Sikhism. In the 19th century the leading western scholars knew that Sikhism was something more than a polity. Before Trumpp and Macauliffe began as the translators of the bani in the Adi Granth, Malcolm and Cunningham had used Sikh literature to understand Sikhism. Actually, the British Sikh Studies turned out to be an interprise in Sikh History and Religion. By the 20th century the Sikh Studies were no longer the exclusive concern of the British. The westernized Indian—scholarship had emerged. But History continued to dominate the Studies. The titles such as 'Guru Nanak in History'[2] (1969) and 'Sikh History and Religion in the Twentieth Century' (1988)[3] appeared. The west-nolonger Europe alone became more active in the area of Sikh Studies. Till date Historiography remains a valid discipline to participate in 'Exploring Sikhism' or in understanding 'Sikhs

1. See, J.S. Grewal, *Contesting Interpretations of the Sikh Tradition* (Manohar, 1998), pp. 23-33.
2. J.S. Grewal, *Guru Nanak in History* (rpt.) (Chandigarh, 1979), The book was first published by the Punjab University in 1969.
3. *Sikh History and Religion in the Twentieth Century,* edited in Toronto by Joseph T.O' Connell and others including J.S. Grewal and W.H. McLeod as the 'visiting editors, (Manohar, 1990).

of the Khalsa'.[4] The Sikh prayer glorifies both the past of Khalsa and the Gurbani'.[5]

This article deals with the foundations of Sikh Studies. Out of the five major western writers on the Sikhs in the 19th century, four have been treated. These are John Malcolm, H.H. Wilson, J.D. Cunningham and M.A. Macauliffe. The 5th was Trumpp. Chronologically, Malcolm's work was published in 1810. Maçauliffe's came out in 1909. Between the two stood H.H. Wilsons (1848) J.D. Cunningham (1849). The century (1810-1909) went a long way to discover Sikhism for the world. Cunningham and Macauliffe left a durable mark upon Sikh Historiography. Trumpp could not. Malcolm became important for he was its real founder.

Cunningham was to be "a source of inspiration for quite a few Indian historians during the twentieth century".[6] This is Professor J.S. Crewal's confession. W.H. McLeod finds it difficult to penetrate the hold of Macauliffe's work over the modern Sikh mind. He writes :[7]

> No other work has so effectively instructed western readers about Sikhism with the result that the Tat Khalsa interpretation of the Sikh faith and community has been firmly fixed in the western understanding.

The West believes, says McLeod, that Sikhism is a unique religion and its true expression is the Khalsa.[8] Try to add a qualifier to these positions and you will be found in 'opposition' to the Sikhs, warns the historian.

---

4. These refer to the two titles brought about by W.H. McLeod by the Oxford University Press in 2000, and 2003, respectively.
5. Max Arthur Macauliffe, *The Sikh Religion,* Vols. V and VI (rpt) (Satvic, 2000), p. 332.
6. J.S. Grewal, Contesting Interpretations, *op. cit.*, p. 33.
7. W.H. McLeod, *Exploring Sikhism* (Oxford, 2000), pp. 261-62.
8. *Ibid.*, p. 262.
9. See Nazer Singh, 'History of Sikh Scriptures Translations : India upto Trumpp', in, *Journal of Sikh Studies,* Vol. XIX, 1995, pp. 22-26.

Who were the Sikhs? This question motivated the British authorities in the late 18th century to gather 'information' about the Singhs or the military strength and other features of Sikh polity. With this originated the Sikh Studies.[9] The undertaking was not so friendly to the Sikhs. In the name of 'independence', it promoted isolation of both the Sikhs and the Punjab from the rest of Hindostan.

What was Sikhism? The Sikh Studies asked this question when the Sikhs were to be administered with European civilization and Christianity by the 19th century. The question widened the scope of Sikh Studies both methodologically and philosophically by admitting Sikh literature including the bani. But it raised the issue of Hindu-Sikh relations.[10]

Who is a Sikh?[11] This is a question for the Sikhs both in the East and the West since the last quarter of the 20th century. The issue of identity is no longer a matter of debate as it was upto the end of 19th century - but has become a contest. At one level, this is a contest for the defence of 'panth de Azad Hasti'. At another level, 'the others' are contesting the authority and right of the Panth to (mis)appropriate to itself the Sikh heritage.

Another pecularity of the British Sikh Studies was that there was a basic methodological and ideological difference between the earily western writings on the Hindus and the Sikhs. While modern Hinduism was discovered from the classical literature, modern Sikhism was found through the political state of Khalsa.[12] Unlike the case of the early Hindus, the British concern with the Sikhs was not a question of civilization or religio-intellectual evolution of Man. It was a concern that was military, diplomatic and political. The 18th century European writers on the Sikhs *viz.* A.L.H. Polier,

10. Trumpp's Translation project (1869-77) raised this question, See, Nazer Singh, *Ibid.*

11. This is the title of W.H. McLeod's book, *Who is a Sikh? The problem of Sikh Identity* (Oxford, 1989).

12. Nazer Singh, 'Khalsa and its Modern Historians', in, *Journal of Sikh Studies,* Vol. XXIII, 1999, pp. 39-40.

George Thomas, Major James Browne and George Forster were literally the agents of the Company. The only exception was Charles Wilkins. But even he failed to arouse the British interest in Sikhism either as a religious or literary tradition. It was in spite of his positive note on 'the Sikh college' and the Books therein at Patna in 1781. Works of Browne and Forster were published in 1789 and 1798, respectively.[13]

The expansion of the Empire upto Delhi politically and upto the Indus diplomatically under Lord Wellesley (1798-1805) and more so the Anglo-Sikh treaties of January 1806 and April 1809 made John Malcolm and Charles Metcalfe interested in the Sikhs.

Conciously, Malcolm expanded the scope of British information agencies into Sikh Studies by including Sikh literature and Punjabi authors. He based his *Sketch of the Sikhs* (1810) on the Adi-Granth and the Dassam Granth as well as on the works of Bhai Gurdass and Mani Singh. He was helped by Leydon, the orientalist. More significant than individuals was the backing of Calcutta that Malcolm enjoyed. This backing was crucial because Calcutta had already a good collection of Punjabi/Sikh manuscripts made by Forster, William Carrey and Colebrook—the preserver of an early/orthodox Janamsakhi.

Sketch of the Sikhs was an exhaustive report on the Sikhs and Sikhism as a religion and polity. Again Malcolm conciously prefered *bani* to show the teachings of the Gurus. In fact, he wanted to show as to how these were actually/originally. He was struck by the fact that Guru Nanak was able to criticize the Hindu and Muslim religious malpractice without creating any big opposition to his own reformation or contributing in any way to the existing hostility between the two communities. For Malcolm, the bani and method of Nanak promoted Hindu-Muslim unity by presenting God as the common source of Hinduism and Islam. Further, Gurū Nanak led both Hindus and Muslims to return to a common worship. Malcolm

13. See Nazer Singh, *Delhi and Punjab Essays in History and Historiography* (New Delhi, 1996), Chp. I.

concluded that Guru Nanak had promised devotion to God and peace to Man. It was Malcom's conviction that History could be an educational tool that was useful for reconciling the Nations.[14]

Impressed by the method and results of Guru Nanak's teachings, Malcolm proposed that a biography of Guru Nanak be compiled on the basis of his bani to judge the Sikh movement as a whole. Till it was accomplished, judgement on this account be postponed, he adviced. To be brief, Malcolm made Guru Nanak and Sikh scriptures relevant for reformation in British India by showing how caste and the practice like Kudi-mar (infanticide) were contrary to the Rahit or Injunctions of Guru Gobind Singh.[15]

Notwithstanding his failure to see the originality of Sikh creed or philosophy, H.H. Wilson[16] treated Guru Nanak as one of the many Bhagti and Sufi reformers. These reformers, he wrote, fashioned a simple faith and worship in which the high and low castes along with the Muslims could "cordially combine", and did learn as to how to "lay aside their uncharitable feelings towards each other". The literature these reformers produced, continued Wilson, was influential with the agricultural population in north India.

Neither Sikh theology nor polity recommended itself to Professor's imagination. Wilson said even the anti-caste instance of Sikhism did't pay in ethical terms. He found the Sikhs highly *demoralized,* and traced this condition to the worship of 'the Book and the Sword'. The Sikhs were just Hindus because even 'the pure Sikh faith' acknowledged the whole scheme of Hindu mythology. For Wilson Udasis and Nirmalas were the only true Sikhs. The little bani used by him were a couple of hymns he had heard at Benaras.

Professor Wilson's interpretation was rejected by

---

14. *Ibid.*

15. Nazer Singh, *Khalsa, op. cit.,* p. 43.

16. See J.S. Grewal, Contesting Interpretations, *op. cit.,* pp. 28-29. Also, The Sikh Religion : A Symposium.

Cunningham. The rejection was complete. First Cunningham made an extensive use of Gurbani and other Sikh writings. Secondly, he elaborated on Malcolm's idea that method of Guru Nanak was relevant for the British India. Thirdly, he assigned a primacy to Sikh ideas and institutions in the making of Sikh movement. History of Sikhism continuously reminded Cunningham the rise of Christianity in the medieval England.

Basing himself on *the Gouree Rag* and *Japji*, Cunningham found how Guru Nanak's concept of Divinity was more lofty than 'the circumscribed divinity' painted by Ramanand and Kabir.[17] Nanak's Lord was the one, the sole, the timeless being; the creator, the self-existent, the incomprehensible and the ever lasting." He likened the Deity to Truth—the eternal truth—that was "ultimate idea or cause of all we know or behold". His addressees were equally the Pandit, Mulla, the Darvesh and the Sanyasi who were advised to remember Lord of Lords who had seen the rise and fall of numberless Muhammads, Vishnus and Shivas. *Asa* showed Cunningham that Guru Nanak treated virtues, charities, heroic deeds and the gathered wisdom fruitless without the knowledge of God. The Guru rebuked those 'vain men who saw eternal life in their own act of faith'. Cunningham noted the grace as an element in Nanak's concept of Divinity. Salvation was a matter of grace. *Prabhati Ragni* is referred to show that good conduct and good works on man's part did matter to God while confering grace.

The *Asa Rag, Suhi* and *Ramkali* are collectively put to give Guru Nanak's view of life. "Life is as the shadow of the passing bird, but the soul of man is, as the potter's wheel, ever circuling on its pivot", says he. Happy was the one 'who remains bright amidst darkness, unmoved amid deciet'. Cunningham did not expect Guru Nanak to speculate upon 'being' or the material world, in the manner of Plato or Vyas.'[18] But the Guru looked for a 'resting place'.

Guru Nanak did't deny Divinity to Muhammad or the

17. J.D. Cunningham, *History of the Sikhs* (Delhi, 1996), p. 38.

18. See Cunningham, *Ibid.*, pp. 38-39.

Hindu incarnations, but he lamented that sin should prevail despite of them. He did't assert a special divinity for himself. But different is the case with his followers who regarded him as the successor to the inspired teachers of the world. Guru Nanak had it the image of a teacher "sent to reclaim fallen mortals of all creeds and countries within the limits of his knowledge". Cunningham further focussed upon this image by saying :[19]

> He rendered his mission applicable to all times and places, yet he declared himself to be but the slave, the humble messenger of the Almighty, making use of universal truth as his sole instrument.

Guru Nanak did't glorify the pious harmit at the cost of a devoted householder. Nor did he participate in the cow-hog controversy. Moreover, he was not a municipal law-giver, in fact his reform was 'religious and moral'. He left 'the social amelioration' and 'political progress' of his followers to the operations of time that meant the care of his successors, maintained Cunningham.

Cunningham refused to accept Wilson's argument that the martial tradition impaired in every way the religious or devotional aspect of Sikhism. Guru Arjun's reforms and Bhai Gurdas's interpretation of the mission of Guru Nanak transformed the idea of 'a gradual fusion of Mohammedans and Hindus into a common observers of a new and a better creed' into an active principle of, and for, the multitude.[20] Guru Nanak was presented as the 'instrument of God for the redemption of the world' as well as the symbol of 'every hope and feeling of the Indian races'.[21] The active faith got an other impulse under Guru Hargobind. It went a long way to separate them from 'all Hindus sects'. After him, the Sikhs "were in little danger of relapsing into the limited merit or utility of monks and mendicants". Guru Teg Bahadur "by his own

19. *Ibid.*, p. 40.
20. *Ibid.*, p. 41.
21. *Ibid.*

example powerfully aided in making the disciples of Nanak a martial as well as a devotional people".[22] An 'authentic composition' the *Vachittar Natak,* talked of the ancient royal background as well as the piety of parents of the 10th Guru.

Cunningham used the *Vachittar Natak, Hazara Sabad, Rahitnamas,* and *Gurbilas* to portray Guru Gobind Singh and the Khalsa. The words *chit an bhaian Hamra awan ko* reminded him Milton's *Paradise Lost.*[23] ('Account me man, I for his sake will leave thy bossom'.) In short, the task of social freedom and political progress of the faithfull was fulfilled by Guru Gobind Singh who 'bestowed upon them a distinct political existence, and inspired them with the desire of being socially free and nationally independent'. For Cunningham, the Sikh faith got itself established through the Khalsa as a prevailing sentiment and guiding principle "to work its way in the world".[24] How would this active faith interact with 'the civilization and christianity of Europe'? Cunningham was not sure, he was rather worrisome on this account. He expected the British to be careful while dealing with the Sikhs. For this, he recorded the predominance of the war-like Singhs in the Punjab and their spread "as soldiers from Kabul to the South of India". The record was meant to show the significance of Sikh tradition for the new rulers.

The greatest western scholar the British Punjab was able to produce was M.A. Macauliffe.[25] For fifteen years he worked on Sikhism, "an unknown religion" to introduce it to the world in the 20th century. Trumpp's failure to do the same was the immediate cause for Macauliffe's undertaking. But it would not be correct to reduce the context of Macauliffe's writings either to Trumpp's failure or the ideological needs and preferences of the Singh Sabha movement. Cunningham had

22. *Ibid.,* p. 59.
23. *Ibid.,* f.n. 03, pp. 61-62.
24. *Ibid.,* p. 80.
25. See, M.A. Macauliffe, *The Sikh Religion,* Vol. I and II PREFACE, iii-xxxiv. Also W.H. McLeod, *Exploring Sikhism,* pp. 257-63 and J.S. Grewal, *Contesting Interpretations,* pp. 43-53.

entertained doubts about the capacity of 'the more learned' (in directly the orientalists like H.H. Wilson and the missionary observers and the British policy makers) to understand Sikh faith and people properly. Macauliffe registered this failure.[26] He desired to understand the Sikhs afresh for he had realized that the Sikh people 'were not understood by their rulers' (McLeod, 2000). It pained him to note that Sikhism was being treated as 'a heathen religion'. Further, the spiritual happiness and loyalty of its professors was seen as a negligible item.[27] He sat to identify the merits of Sikhism for both the Empire and the human civilization.

The list of 'religious and moral' merits of Sikhism as made by Macauliffe was fairly long.[28] Sikhism put prohibition on idolatory, hypocracy, caste exclusiveness, descrimination against women, use of the intoxicants, tobacco-smoking, infanticide, slander, pilgrimages to the sacred rivers and tanks of Hindus. Positively it inculcated loyalty, gratitude for the favour received, philanthropy, justice, impartiality and other virtues 'known to the honest citizen of any country'. For Macauliffe, to take Sikhs as Hindus was to act in opposition to the teachings of the Gurus.

Curiously Macauliffe noticed that 'the greatest religious reformers' of the world had not come from the ranks of clergy but from the laity.[29] These included Pythagoras, Isaiah, Moses, Socrates, Budha, Christ, 'Muhammad of Makka', Kabir and Nanak. Macauliffe said 'divine emotionalism' was given the loftiest hights by Guru Nanak. Also the Guru exalted his mental vision to an ethical ideal beyond the conception of Hindu or Mohammedan.[30] Nor was this ideal affected in any way 'by Semitic and Christian influence'. The originality of Sikhism was in its 'more comprehensive ethical system'.

---

26. McLeod, Exploring Sikhism, p. 259.
27. Quoted in McLeod, *Ibid.*, p. 262.
28. *The Sikh Religion,* Vol. I, PREFACE xxiii.
29. *Ibid.*, INTRODUCTION, liv.
30. *Ibid.*, liv-lv.

To sum up, the European writers laidown the foundations of Modern Sikh Historiography. The British Sikh Studies beginning with John Malcolm constituted the earlier phase of this historiographical tradition.The tradition gave due importance to Sikh literature especially the Sikh Scriptures and chronicles. The 'friendly' diplomatic and political Anglo-Sikh relations objectively helped Malcolm to present Guru Nanak as a great reformer. Guru Nanak's life and message were found relevant and useful. Devotion to God and peace to man were the essentials of the Guru's mission, recorded Malcom. This interpretation was in line with his conviction that historical knowledge could reconcilitate the nations and races. Logically, Guru Nanak was projected as a promoter of Hindu Muslim unity.

Inspite of his concern for the civil ideas and institutions of the Sikhs, H.H. Wilson failed to see the originality of Guru Nanak's mission or the uniqueness of his method and teachings. Failure was caused by his inability to see the Sikhs through their scriptures. Khalsa did not appeal to Professor Wilson's imagination. J.D. Cunningham was right in observing that the too much learned of the West were likely to misread Sikhism.

Cunningham made an extensive use of Bani and other Sikh literature. He developed the idea of Guru Nanak as the great reformer. Moreover he treated Sikh ideas and institutions as the makers of Sikh movement. Cunningham was loud in proclaiming the uniqueness of Sikhism—Sikhism was unique not only for Guru Nanak's method of presenting Divinity but also for its social practice culminating into the Khalsa. The Sikhs under Guru Arjan, Guru Hargobind and Guru Teg Bahadur were martial and devotional people. Khalsa inherited these qualities. The tenth Guru entitled the Sikhs to 'be socially free and nationally independent'. Like Guru Nanak, (Guru) Khalsa could act as an 'instrument of God for the redemption of the whole world' as well as the symbol of 'every hope and feeling of the Indian races'. Cunningham stood by the unity of Sikh Gurus. He relied on Bhai Gurdass and the Vachittar Natak to present Sikhism. It was through Khalsa that the Sikhs established themselves 'to work through the world'. For Cunningham the Sikh polity stood for 'social amelioration and national independence'. The overpowered Singhs as the bearers of both a living faith and active patriotism were Cunningham's worry. He expected the British as the carriers of European civilization and Christianity to deal with the Singhs carefully.

M.A. Macauliffe started from where Cunningham had left. He was convinced that Sikhism was in crises. The Sikhs were known to the world only as a military class. Sikhism as a religion was 'practically unknown'. Moreover, it was still being regarded as a Heathean religion. The British rulers were the least inclined to see it as a source of Sikh spiritualism and happiness. Macauliffe wanted the rulers to improve their reading of Sikhism. Both the empire and civilization could't afford the relapse of Sikhs into Hinduism. The historian was sure that the Sikhs were't Hindus. Teachings of the Gurus did't admit them to be otherwise, he wrote. Likewise, Guru Nanak's ethical ideal had nothing to do with the Semetic and Christian influence. Macauliffe was hopeful that the 'enlightened nations' would not allow Sikhism to perish provided these might be informed of 'the merits of Sikhism'. He choose to act as an ambassdor of Sikhism.

Appendices

APPENDIX-I

Copy of Mr. McLeod's Letter Dt. 21st February, 1859

To

R.H.Davies Esquire,
Secretary to Government,
Punjab and its dependencies,
Dated Lahore the 21st February, 1859

Sir,

With a letter No. 4568 dated 13th November 1857 from the Secretary to the Government of India, the Chief Commissioner of the Punjab received copy of Despatch from the Honourable the Court of Directors, in the Public Department, No. 111 Dated 12th August 1857, approving of a suggestion made to them by Mr. R.N. Cust; that a correct copy of the Grunth or Sacred Book of the Sikhs should be procured, and a translation made of it into English, or some other European language.

This letter and inclosure were referred to me with a request that after consulting with such of the most influential Sikhs, as I might think proper; I would indicate the course. It might appeare to me advisable to adopt.

I have the honour to return the above documents and to state, that, I have now in my possession, an authentic copy of all the "Grunths" made our to me by "Guru" Sadhu Singh Sodhi of Kartarpur, the chief of the Sodhi priesthood; the representatives of Guru Gobind all the natives with whom I consulted, indicated him as the proper party to supply a copy as he possessed the originals, written or signed by the Gurus themselves and could at once have them faithfully transcribed and on my applying to him he promised to have this done.

Accordingly in fulfilment of this promise, he sent to me, some time ago, conveyed in his own state bullock carriage or Rath, a copy of the 'adi Grunth' or precepts of the first 5 Gurus compiled by Guru Arjan and a short time ago the remaining volume, designated the Daswan Padshah da Grunth, or book of the 10th leader/Guru Gobind/was made over by him to the Deputy Commissioner of Jullundhar, with which district, Kartarpur is situated, from whence it has been recently farwarded to Lahore.

My request of the Guru was that he would have copies made by transcribers, whom Government would renumerate for the task, but although, he at the time made no objection, he now altogether declines this—stating that he has presented them himself out of respect and deference to the British Government. He has also since informed me that so great a privilige has been always attached by him to the possession of the only true originals that although Maharaja Ranjeet Singh had expressed a desire to obtain a copy taken direct from them, he had refused give one. It will, I think, be suitable if he receive from the proper quarter, a recognization of this act of compliance.

I would now suggest that those two volumes which I have had filled into a suitable box, be sent to England for deposit in the Oriental Library belonging to Her Majesty, and it would in my opinion be most appropriate that Sir John Lawrence, should himself present them on their reaching England. By their being thus disposed of, not only will a valuable addition be made to the manuscripts of the above library but the very best opportunity will be afforded to the oriental scholars of Europe, who may be so inclined to study the book and render it into English or other European language.

In India the "Gurmukhi language and character do not appear to have been taken up by any of our oriental scholars with interest, and I know of no one here who possesses the requisite knowledge, inclination and leisure for the task of making a translation. I would strongly recommend, therefore, as the preferable course, that the scholars of England, and of continental countries, be invited to undertake the task on which they would bring to bear philosophical appliances and opportunities and an amount of oriental research and learning not to be looked far here.

If however, it be desired that the translation be undertaken in India; ordinary copies of the Grunths and men to explain them are readily procurable and it has been suggested that the readiest mode would be, to have it first translated into English. Mr. Cust is quite preferred to have this plan put into execution if the requisite funds be placed at his disposal and as he has peculiar tastes and aptitudes far such an undertaking, was himself the original proposer of the—scheme, and is now located at Amritsar the headquarters of the Sikhism, it would not be trusted to better hands.

Another mode in which the same object might perhaps be obtained would be by an offer of a certain sum/say Rs. 1000/ far a good translation of the Grunths, when some of our officers or other individuals, who may have the taste and the leisure for oriental pursuits, would perhaps qualify themselves for the tasks, and compete for the honour and reward thus held out.

Source : Proceedings Foreign Deptt., 8th April, 1859, no. 142 (N.A.I.).

APPENDIX-2

Office Note

From Punjab Government

Dated 8 Feb. 1872.

Rentention of Dr. Trumpp's services to translate the Granth of Govind Singh.

In 1857 the Court of Directors, under a suggestion by Mr. Cust desired the Government of India to consider in what way a copy and careful translation might be made of the Granth, or sacred Book of the Sikhs, as it was undoutedly desirable that the Government of India should become acquainted with a work which regulates the principles and opinions, morale and religious, of so large section of population of British India.

The opinion of the Punjab Government was invited by the Government of India.

In reply [No. 117-245, dated Ist March 1859, Consultation, 8th April 1859, No. 141-43], the chief Commissioner forwarded a letter from the Financial Commissioner stating that he had obtained an athuentic copy of the Adi Granth and the Daswan Padshah Ka Granth from Guru Sadhu Singh Sodee of Kartarpur, Jallundhar, Chief of the priesthood, who possessed the original, and he recommended that the works should be sent England for deposit in the Oriental Library and translation by competent linguists.

The Books were sent to England under the care of Mr. Prinspp, and a suitable Khillut was presented to the Guru.

In 1869 the Lieutenant Governor suggested [No. 164-62 dt. 25th May 1869, Gen. A, July, 1869, No. 68-69] that the enquiry be made whether any thing had been done towards their translation. This was accordingly done, and it was suggested to the Home Government that, if it was found impossible to have it done in England the translation should be made here.

In reply [No. 284 dt. 21st Dec. 1869, Gen. A, Feb. 1870 No.

11-13] the Secretary of State forwarded copy of correspondence with Dr. Trumpp, of Hullingen, Wurtemberg, who undertook the translation on the understanding that he was to receive £ 300 per annum for three years in Europe from first November 1869, and £ 500 for one year and half from first November 1872, if he found it necessary to proceed to India for its completion, his expenses (£ 200) to and fro being paid him.

In May 1870 [No. 62 dt. 31st May 1870, Proceedings, Gen. A, 1870, July No. 67] the Secretary of State forwarded a copy of further correspondence with Dr. Trumpp, who had underestimated the difficulty of the work at first.

Under the new arrangement than made, it was agreed that Dr. Trumpp should proceed to India as early as possible on a salary of £ 500 for the first year, and of £ 400 for the second, that he should receive the assistance of two competent Sikh Moonshis and that for following 2½ years, whilst pursuing the work of translation in English, he should receive £ 300 per annum, his passage money being given as before. The original sum of £ 1,850 was not be exceeded and the arrangement was to be final [From Secretary of State to Dr. Trumpp dt. 26 March 1870, Gen. A, July 1870, No. 67-70].

In Dec. 1870 Dr. Trumpp reported his arrival on the 10th December at Bombay en-route for Lahore.

In September 1871 he represented that, unless a salary of £ 500 was allowed him for the second year of his stay instead of the £ 400 originally agreed upon, and an allowance of Rs. 200 given him for his expenses to Simla in the post hot season he would be compelled to throw up his appointment and return to England, as the expenses of living in India had become so much dearer than 12 years before. He also offered to stay another year on the above terms to translate the Granth of Govind Singh, which throws considerable light on the political principles and constitution of the Khalsa Sikhs. The increase was granted, and the offer accepted [Dt. 12 Dec. 1871, Gen. A. Dec. 1871 No. 20-23].

Between January 1871 and January 1872, some demi

officials correspondence passed between Dr. Trumpp and the Foreign Secretary as to the difficulties of the work and the intended resignation of the Doctor.

In his letter of 25th April 1871, latter states that if had to rely on the Sikh Granthis alone, he would be utterly lost, as not one of them had the slightest knowledge of the grammer. The difficulty in the translation lays in the fact that the language of the Granth is the old Punjabi of two or three hundred years ago, and consists of a number of dialectics of all the northern portion of India down to Behar, and as far westward as Sind. Most of the language is faulty and barbarous, and thousands of words are now absolete. On the whole, the Doctor was sorry he undertook the work, which he characterized a very poor literary composition, but interesting in a philological point of view. He was obliged to make his own grammer and dictionary as he proceeded, and he observed that Indian philologists would be surprised when they see the grammer of the Granth. He expressed a doubt whether he should complete the materials for translation within the two years prescribed, as the difficulties were really great, consisting as the work did of such a motley mixture of languages which defied the most careful investigation. He did not understand what Sir McLeod meant by a "Popularized Translation". A translation is either corret or incorrect. If merely a traditional explantions were given, the translation would be senseless and would answer no purpose.

On the 30th December 1871, that is, a few days after he received the sanction to his application for an increase of salary, Dr. Trumpp reported his resignation and withdrawl from the translation of the Granth of Govind Singh, unless it was expressively understood that two years would be allowed him to elaborate its translation in England on a salary £ 300 per annum in addition to the one year allowed him for its preparation here, and the two and a half allowed for the elaboration of the Adi Granth. He proposed to leave India by the end of February 1872.

On the 11th January 1872, Mr. Griffin wrote :

"Dr. Trumpp has expressed great unwillingness to go on with the translation of the Granth of Govind Singh for the reason that he does not understand the Government has allowed him sufficient time for the work's completion in a satisficatory manner." He added "we are very anxious to keep Dr. Trumpp, who is a most valuable man, and were hoping to be able to utilize him as a Pushtoo Professor, of which language he is one of the best living authorities."

The Punjab Government now forwards a letter dt. 29th January, from the Doctor, agreeing to take up the translation on the condition :

(I) That for the current year an additional salary of Rs. 300 per mensem be allowed him, for which addition he would superintendent the Oriental School, the Punjab University, and lecturer on Sanskrit, Prakrit, Persian, Pushtoo & Co., provided that he would not be required to give more than two lectures a day.

(II) That after the expiration of the current year, two additional years be allowed him to work out the translation on a salary of £ 300 per annum.

(III) That three months' leave be granted him during the hot months, to spare his health for the translation.

The Doctor states that after expiration of the current year, he would stay in India, if his salary, from whatever source, should not be less than Rs. 700 per mensem.

The Lieutenant Governor is anxious to retain his services in the Punjab where his knowledge of Sanskrit, Sindhi, Punjabi and Pushtoo makes him especially valuable. His honour purposes to utilize him for Pushtoo and Punjabi lectures and examinations, that the preparation of improved mannuals of those languages, while he can also be engaged as Sanskrit lecturer at the University College, Lahore.

The Lieutenant-Governor would therefore accede to the Doctor's terms, and make up his income to Rs. 700 per mensem, the extra expense to be borne by the Punjab Government and desires an answer by telegraph as the Doctor is anxious to make his arrangements. From the demi-official correspondence it appears that Dr. Trumpp has completed his preparations for the full translation of the Adi Granth in one year, instead of the two allowed him, see his letter dt. 30th December 1871. It is not shown how he proposes to complete the translation.

Source : Proceedings, For-Gen., A, 1872, nos. 110-114 (N.A.I.).

APPENDIX-3

Doctor Trumpp's translation of the Adi Granth and the Granth of Guru Govind Singh of the Sikh Community

"In 1857 the Court of Directors desired the Government of India to consider in what way a copy and careful translation might be made of the Granths or sacred books of the sikhs.

The Book Adi Granth and Daswan Padshah Ka Granth, were sent to England and in November 1869 Dr. Trumpp undertook to translate them in 4½ years at a cost not exceeding £ 1850.

In September 1871, the Doctor represented that unless his salary was increased he would be compelled to throw up his appointment and return to England; but at the same time offered to stay in India another year and translate the Granth of Govind Singh. His offer was accepted and the increase granted.

Please See, K.W. Proceedings, Gen. A, AP. 1872, Nos. 110-114.

In January 1872, however, the Doctor expressed unwillingness to go on with the translation of the Granth of Govind Singh, saying that Government had not given him sufficient time to complete the work satisfactorily, but as the Punjab Government was anxious to secure his services, they agreed to extend the time to 7½ years, and to make his income upto Rupees 700 a month, bearing themselves the extra expenses.

"For Particulars about the expenses, please see Secretary's remarks on the Previous Note[1], within field.

Dr. Trumpp, however, left for Europe without completing[2] the translation of the Adi Granth, and the Proposal of the Punjab Govt. did not take effect.

The secretary of state was requested to report from time to time the progress made by the Doctor in the work in question. He in December 1872 last reported that Dr. Trumpp complained much of the great sacrifices he had made in accepting the work and the pecuniary disadvantage in which he was placed thereby, and stated that it would take 2½ years more to work out the final translation of the Adi Granth, of Govind Singh's Granth, he said that the translation of the whole Granth would be a useless undertaking, for Govind sing was only acknowledged by a very small portion of the sikh

(1) K.W. Proceeding AP. 1872, No. 110-14

(2) Before the question was decided

community; he considered the Rahitnamas of Govind singh, which contains the constitution of the Sikh Khalsa, of far greater importance and offered to translate them observing 'if Her Majesty's Government should wish the whole Granth be translated, I would beg that this work be entrusted to some one else, as I would see no end to my labours?

Mr. Grote[3] concurred in the opinion of the Doctor, but Mr. D. McLeod considered it most important that the whole of the Grunth should be translated.

(3) of the Bengal civil service

Mr. Crust proposed that Dr. Trumpp might finish the Adi Granth and the Rahitnamas, and a committee composed of Sikh, Hindu and European gentlemen, be formed for translating the whole Granth.

The Secretary of state asked the opinion of this Government on the point in question after reference being made to the Lieutenant-Governor, Punjab.

The Punjab Government was accordingly requested to given an opinion on the subject." [After this the Note contained the summary of Mr. Thornton letter of 14th July.]

"In June last", [continue the Note,] "the Secretary of state forwarded further papers connected with the translation of the Adi Granth and an estimate of the cost[4] of printing it, and requested that the Punjab Govt. may be consulted regarding the desirability of printing the whole or a portion of the work.

(4) Proceed. Gen. A, July 1873, No. 34-37

"The Punjab Government was called upon for an early report. This has not yet arrived.

"Perhaps the Punjab Report may be awaited and the whole question taken up at once."

C.N.N. 30-7-73. "In reality the sikh scriptures are sealed books and no one knows anything about them. I think it would be a standing disgrace to the British Government to grudge £ 1,136 for the Publication of the Adi Granth. The whole should be printed in extenso. With regard to Govind's Granth, only those parts which are said to be written by the Guru himself should be translated (as is suggested by Trumpp) together with the two Rahitnamas-C.U.A. "I quite agree with Mr. Aitchison as to the Adi Granth, and am able to say that General Cunningham coincides also. I am affraid Dr. Trumpp is not wholly reliable as to time, and possibly as to expense, but any way the limits to which he is likely to go as to either are not likely to prove extravagent, and he is the only man who could do the work at present available."

E.C. Bayley. 2.9.73
Source : Progds. For-Gen., A, Sep. 1873, nos. 6-10 (N.A.I.).

APPENDIX-4

De-Railling the Translation Project-I
The Issue of Making a choice between the Rahitnamas and the Dassam Granth

"From

T.H. Thornton Esll.
Secretary to Govt. of Punjab and Its Dependencies

To

C.U. Aitchison
Secretary to Govt. of India,
Foreign Deptt.
dated 14th July 1873"

"Sir,

In your letter No. 477 G, dated 21st February forwarding copy of Secretary of State's despatch No. 140 dated 31st December, 1872, with reference on the subject of the proposed translation of the Adi Granth, you required with reference to para 3 of the despatch, the opinion of the Hon'able the Lieutenant-Governor as to whether the Rahitnamas of Guru Gobind merit translation in preference to the book known as the Granth of the 10th Padshah."

"2. The Hon'able the Lieutenant-Governor, the receipt of your letter, caused enquiries to be made through the Director of Public Instruction from the Lahore Anjuman (A Native Literary Society) and the principal Granthis of Amritsar and Lahore and also from Sardar Atar Singh of Bhadour, in Patiala territory, a member of the senate of the Punjab university college, and perhaps the most learned of the Sikh aristocracy."

"3. I have now the honour to forward copy of a letter No. 154, dated 30th June, from the officiating Director of Public Instruction in this province, with enclosure containing the information called for, and also translation of a reply received from Sardar Atar Singh. From these documents it will be perceived that the General opinion of the Lahore, and Amritsar Granthis, as well as of the late Sardar Sir Nehal Singh, Chacchi, K.C. s. 9, is that of the two works the Granth is more important, and should be preferentially translated; while Pandit Radha Kishan and Bhai Budh Singh assert that the rules of Rahitnamas are far from strictly observed by the Sikhs of the present day. On the other hand, Sardar Attar Singh, Bhadour, entirely concurs in the views of Dr. Trumpp."

"4. His Honour, I am desired to say, is inclined to attach more weight to the opinion of Sardar Atar Singh, agreeing, as it does, with the opinion of Dr. Ernest Trumpp, than to the opinion of the other authorities above mentioned, and would recommend that the translation of the Rahitnamas have the preference; but that, if possible, those portions of the Granth of the 10th Padshah which relate to the religious precepts of doctorine of the Sikh religion be translated also."

"I have the honour to be
Sir,
your most obedient servant
Secretary to Government of
Punjab".

Source : Progds. For-Gen., A, Sep. 1873, no. 6, (N.A.I.).

APPENDIX-4A

Justifying the De-Railling of the Translation Project-I

Extract from the letter of C. Pearson referred to by T.H. Thornton as No. 154 dated 30th June, 1873.

"Before Dr. Trumpp left India I had opportunities of conversing with him upon the subject of the Second Granth (that of Guru Govind Singh, the tenth Padshah), and I have now consulted Pandit Radha Kishan and Bhai Budh Singh (who was referred to by Sir Donald MacLeod) upon the relative value of the Granth and the Rahitnamas. Pandit Radhakishan whose opinion I consider of much value, as it is uninfluenced by any religious bias, says the Sikhs of the present day disregard the Rahitnamas because they have given up the strict observance of the customs enjoyed therein. He thinks that the Sikhs are guided almost entirely by an oral tradition, and that their scriptures have no practicle influence upon their manner of life."

"Bhai Budh Singh complains that people are now without knowledge, and learn all the religion by word of mouth. He thinks Rahitnamas were written by different persons about forty years after the death of Guru Govind Singh. At the time when they were composed the people acted up to the strict rules contained in them, but the books and rules have now both gone out of fashion."

"The result of the present enquiry seems to be that the Sikhs have invented sacred books rather in imitation of the scriptures of other religions than because the spirit of their religion lived in written traditions. But the Sikh literature contains the history of Sikh religion, and so for, portions of the Granths and of the Rahitnamas deserve to be studied and explained".

C. Pearson

Source : Progds. For-Gen., A, Sep., 1873, no. 7 (N.A.I.).

APPENDIX-4B

Justifying the De-Railling of Translation Project-II Choosing between the Dassam Granth and the Rahitnamas

"Letter of Atar Singh (Translation of)"
"Dated 30 March, 1873.
From—Sardar Atar Singh of Bhadour
To—Secy to Govt. of Punjab".
"After compliments :

"Your letter dated 18th March 1873 was received at Bhadour by the Patiala Post on the 27th instant. I was than absent from Bhadour, and my reply has been delayed on this account. I am extremely obliged to His Honor the Lieutenant Governor for his having asked my opinion, and beg to say that I concur with the opinion of Dr. Ernest Trumpp, *i.e.*, it would be useless and would secure no purpose to translate the whole of the Grunth of the Daswan Padshah. It is very important without doubt to translate the Rahitnamas only".

Source : For-Gen., A, Sep. 1873, no. 9 (N.A.I.).

APPENDIX-5

Further De-Railling the Translation Project-I
Extracts from Trumpp's Letter

"Dated Tubingen, 13th January 1873"
"From Dr. E. Trumpp"
"To under-Secretary of State for India, India Office London"

"I beg to forward to you (Via Hamburg) the first portion of the translation of the Adi Granth which is now progressing day by day."

"The Grunth of the Sikhs turn out a very different book from what it was hitherto supposed to be".

"It contains no deism nor a mixture of Hinduism and Mohammedanism as so often stated, but teaches throughout and with full consequence the common Hindu Pantheism as set forth in the Vedant and in Bhagavat-gita.

"The language of the Granth is very difficult, not only on account of the great many words which have now absolete, and which must be found out by a wearisome process of comparision with the Sanscrit and Prakrit, but more so on account of the confused and intericate style used in these poetical effusions."

[This is followed by two more Paras on the style of the compositions in the Adi Granth. Trumpp is derogatory in his remarks on particularily the style of the Sikh Gurus. Hence these two paras stand ommitted here—Nazer Singh]

"The greatest part of the Granth contains a sort of devotional hymns, rather poor in conception, clumsy in style, and wearisome to read, as the same thought is repeated in a thousand different ways".

"The doctorine set forth is on the whole very meager and not given systematically, but incidently by random remarks. The moral system is hardly touched, and does not rise above the level of the common Hindu morality."

[Here again comes a para on the style and erudition of the

Sikh Gurus. The para downgrades the Gurus. Here it is left out—Nazer Singh]

"The writtings of the old Hindu Bhagatas (or devotees) are on the whole far superior to those of the Sikh Gurus themselves as regards contents and style, especially those of Kabir from whom Nanak and his successors have borrowed all they know and preach."

"In fact so much is clearly seen from the Granth itself, that the Sikh Gurus taught nothing new whatever, and if a separate religious system and partly a new nationality has in course of time sprung up from it, this is not owing in any way to the doctorine taught by them but to their financial and political organization, which they gave to their disciples, and to the weakness of the Mugal Government".

"Though I cannot help expressing my individual opinion that the contents of the Granth by no means justify the high repute in which it is held in India yet it is undoubtedly of great value from a philological point of view, as it is, to say so, a great store-house of a variety of Hindu dialects of the middle ages, of which we elsewhere would have had no trace. It fills up a gap in our knowledge of the development of the North Indian Vernacular, which must be most welcome to the philologer. Our great and best acquisition from the study of the Granth will be a grammar of the idoms contained therein by which the modern arian languages will receive their due light".

"Towards the end of March I hope to have progressed with my translation so for that a volume of 500-600 pages could be printed provided that Gurmukhi types are to be had in England for the purpose".

"I am drawing also out a life of Nanak from original Sikh sources which could be added as an introduction to the translation of the Granth, together with the remarks on the compositions of the Granth".

Source : Progds. For-Gen., A, July 1873, no. 35 (N.A.I.).

APPENDIX-5A

Further De-Railling the Translation Project-2

"Note by the Librarian [India Office, Library] on the first installment of Dr. Trumpp's translation of the adi-Granth".

"Dr. Trumpp appears to have taken great pains with his translation, and it may be presumed that the latter is true and trustworthy reflex of the original work. It is evident however that it would little repay the trouble of reading through it so much does it teem with repititions and trivialities of every kind. As a translation therefore of an ordinary oriental book it would not be worth the expenses of printing, and an abstract or selection of the most telling passages might sufice."

"But it stands to reason whether it may not be found desirable from political considerations to have a printed translation of the whole body of the sacred code of the Sikhs".

"The translator's notes are invaluable and form a rich store of the most varied and original information on every subject connected with the history and creed of the Sikhs".

"In the event of its being thought desirable to have the translation together with Introduction and Notes, printed in extenso. I have obtained an estimate of the maximum cost, which I herewith enclose.

"12th March, 1873" "Sd. R. Rost"

Source : For-Gen., A, July 1873, no. 36 (N.A.I.).

APPENDIX-5B

Further De-Railling the Translation Project-3

Summary of the letter of Secretary of State for India, 4th June 1873, to Govt. of India, Informing the latter about the view of R. Rost, the Librarian of India office Library.

The Secretary of State drew the attention of Govt. of India to the negative opinion expressed by R. Rost about the literary value of the Adi Granth. Rost was "advers to the printing of the work, from a purely literary point of view".

The State Secretary was of the view that the Punjab Govt. should be consulted before investing 'the huge sum' of £ 985.15 (for 300 copies) on the publication of the translation made by Trumpp. Was there a political need to have the whole Adi Granth translated and printed? Could't the 'all useful objects' be secured by printing and publication of judiciously selected extracts of the work, with a connecting link in the form of an abstract of the ommitted passage? The Punjab Govt. was to be ordered to discuss these two proposal with her 'officers, Native gentlemen and Grunthis' and to report back her opinion."

Source : Progds. For-Gen., A, July 1873, no. 37 (N.A.I.).

APPENDIX-6

Justifying the Further De-Railling of Tran. Project-I "Copy of Notes of Conversation held with a view of ascertain if the Adi Granth throws any light on the political history of the Sikhs."

"Bhai Budh Singh[1] says the Granths (especially the Adi Granth) contain matters relating only to the worship of God. The Rahitnamas encourage war against the Mussalmans, and lay down rules for conducting wordly business, private and public."

"Nothing but a piety could be learnt from a translation of the Granths. The Sikh Sardars were wordly men, who cared only for their own aggrandigement, they were ignorant and careless of spiritual things. God only knows how the Sikh empire grew up. It had nothing to do with the Sikh religion. "Bhai Partab Singh[2] says that the Adi Granth contains nothing but spiritual religion. In the second Granth there is a description of weapons, but no order to wear them. Sikhs are divided into classes, the clergy and laymen."

"But Empire is the work of God. The Granths were never used, like the Quran, to stir up religious war. It is evident that the Sikhs forsook their religion, or their kingdom would have not taken away. When the Sikh power was increasing the Sardars must have kept the faith. There is no harm in pilgrimage, but it is of no use. If any virtue is supposed to belong to it, that is heresay.

"Images are to be thrown into the river. Pictures of Krishan and Muhammad are wrong. It is not right to follow the customs of the Hindus. Some Sikhs do, but owing to their ignorance and wickedness."

"Rai Mul Sing (a Minister of the Sikh Government before the annexation) says that the Granths are only concerned with Sikh religion, a translation would throw no light upon the

"(1) Bhai Budh Singh is very old man, be says 86 years.

"(2) Bhai Pratap Singh is perhaps 35 years old.

history of the Sikh Empire. The Sikhs used Hindu law (Dharm Sastras) for themselves, and the shrait for the Mussalmans. No public business was transacted with reference to the Grunths. Maharaja Ranjit Singh used to have the histories of the Mugal kings read to him and followed their practice at his own discretion. He would adopt good advice from the books of any religion. The Khalsa were all Sikhs but in the auxiliary forces he used to have Sikh officers over Mussalman soldiers, and Mussalmans over Sikhs and Hindustanees. He used to make all classes of Hindu, Sikhs continually, and gave much attention to religion at stated times, as the Europeans go to church on Sunday; but political business was one thing and religion an other."

"I asked if there was any difference between Sikhs and Hindus, a Brahmin and two Bhais were present."

"The Question caused embarrassment. Rai Mul Singh said that whatever was right and proper was lawful. Maharaja Ranjeet Singh had treated Brahmins honourably.

"They considered Dr. Trumpp's translation all wrong. He had persisted in giving his own meaning to passages and would not listen to the interpretations of the Bhais."

"Pundit Radhakishan (hereditary chief of the Brahmans of the Punjab, perhaps 70 years old, very intelligent and respectable) said that the Granths were purely religious books and contained no harm so far, but there was nothing to be learnt from them. Neither Nanak nor Govind Singh were anything else but good Hindus. In later times low caste men called themselves Bhais, it was a ridiculous assumption, but there was nothing heretical in it. The Kukas had invented a religion of their own which they said they got out of the Granths. They put aside the Hindu religion entirely, and had their own ceremonies for marriage and funerals. It was a wicked and contemptible heresy, but by the good fortune of the Sarkar, their light had been put out. The idea of the Kukas was quite knew. The Granths had nothing to do with it, and a translation could give no help to understand it. The Kukas imagined that they would found a great surprise. The Hindus do not care for the Granths, but had no objection to them."

"Harbhagat Singh[1] says that there is no system of religion in the Granths, they inculcate, merely pious sentiments. Bhahmins are "required to perform marriage and funeral ceremonies, but that is all. The Sikhs held the same belief as the Hindus about the twenty four avtars ... the sin of the Kukas is that they have rejected the Dharam sastras, that is, the ceremonial law of the Hindus, which is binding upon the Sikhs in matters relating to marriages, funerals, property etc."

"As regards belief in God and morals, the Kookas hold the same opinion as the orthodox Sikhs, but they think they will all go to their Guru in paradise after death, whereas the orthodox believe that men will go to heaven or hell according to their deserts"

Source : Progds. For-Gen., A, January 1874, no. 3 (N.A.I.).

(1) About fifty years old.

APPENDIX-6A

Justifying the Further De-Railling of Trans. Project-02 Extract from the enquiry made by Pearson about the Adi Granth as ordered by the Govt. To know if it would be politically worth to print the whole Granth.

"On the whole, then I am of opinion that the political objects to be attained by the publication of the Adi Granth might be equally secured by the printing and publication of extracts. Obviously there are very large portions of the work which have no political bearing or to put it differently, it would appear that there are very few portions of the Adi Granth which have any political bearing at all. The book is revered and worshipped almost as itself a divinity, and it, and not the Daswan Padshah Ka Granth, is the book to be found in every educated Sikh's house and most generally in Sikh Dharmsalas throughout the land (Sirdar Dyal Singh remarked to me that while hundred of Adi Granth are to be found in privates houses in Amritsar, there might not be ten copies of the Daswan Padshah Ka Granth)".

Source : Progds. For-Gen., A, January 1874, no. 5 (N.A.I.).

APPENDIX-6B

Pearson Interviews Khem Singh Bedi
Method and Objective of the Inquiry made by Pearson

"Copy of Notes of a conversation with Baba Khem Singh, not held with reference to this enquiry."

"Baba Khem Singh is the final descendant of the Sikh Gurus, and is head of the Sikh religion. He is about 40 years old, very intelligent, and liberal in his views. Within certain limits his wish is law to the Sikhs and a large number of Hindus in the Punjab."

"Baba Khem Singh says that the Sikh religion is simply the service of God and the practice of virtue. All men-Christians, Mussalmans, Hindus—may belong to this religion. A large proportion of the Mussalmans of the Punjab are Sikhs at heart (I do not think this is the case—C. Pearson) all that is good in all religions is equally acceptable to God. The Gurus taught what was revealed to them as regards customs. There are two classes of Sikhs—Sikhs, the followers of Baba Nanak, and Singhs, the disciples of Guru Govind Singh. There is no antagonism between Sikhs and Singhs. I asked what did he think of the Koran? He said it was a good book so for as it contained pure religion".

"I said that I had found schools in which Hindu boys read Gurmukhi and were taught moral percepts from the Granth. He said this was common everywhere, because the Sikh priests taught only pure religion. Everyone who became a Sikh did not necessarily take the 'Pahal' (initiation). Most of the Hindus, and Mussalmans of the Punjab were Sikhs at heart. When I went to see him I met him leaving his house on a shooting excursion. He called his sons, two little boys, one of whom can read some urdu and Persian, is to go to the Mission School at Rawalpindee to learn English. I do not speak to him about the Kukas, or the position of Hinduism in the religion of orthodox Sikhs, or the bearing of the Granth upon the political history of the Sikhs".

"Baba Khem Singh corroborated what the Bhai said of the

Rahitnamahs, *viz.*, that they were compiled 40 years after Govind Sing's death and were considered of less authority than the Granths".

Sd/-
C. Pearson
Officiating Director Public
Instructions, Punjab.

Source : Progds. For-Gen., A, January 1874, no. 4 (N.A.I.).

APPENDIX-7

Janamsakhi V.S. the Scriptures
The Translation Project put on New-Lines

Note—Trumpp's Letter dated 26 Nov., 1873 to the Under-Secretary of State for India, shows how the translator proposed to finish his job of translating the Adi Granth and Dassam Granth by producing a book of History and religion. He suggested that volume one of the proposed book should comprise of about 1/3 of the translated Adi Granth with him. For a better understanding of 'the religion of the Sikhs' the book might have the life sketches of the Sikh Gurus. He revealed that he could produce 'The Biography of Nanak' based upon 'the oldest' Janamsakhi.—Nazer Singh.

Trumpp's opinion about the Janaksakhi, he had, is reflected from the following extract from his Letter :

"[The oldest Janaksakhi] differs very considerably from the Janamsakhis now current among the Sikhs, and gives many important hints as to the formation of myths about Nanak and his subsequent deification. The manuscript in question is No. 1728 of the India office Library, and is written in old Gurmukhi characters and in a now antiquated language. To this I shall add extracts from the other Janamsakhis for the sake of comparision so that we shall get for the first time a biography of Nanak DRAWN FROM ORIGINAL SIKH SOURCES (original is the emphasis—N.S.)."

"The Biography of Nanak should be followed by a short-sketch of the life of the other nine Gurus."

"I intend also give some notice on the composition, arrangement, style and meters of the Granth, to which I will be adding a survey of the teaching of the Granth. This last, however, I cannot do before the first volume be printed, that I may be able to refer to it".

[Following this he suggested that his second volume may cover 200-250 pages but the Government would be free to publish or not to publish it. As to the remaining part of the Adi Granth and its publication, Trumpp wrote -]

"I, for my own part, would not advise it, for reasons I have repeatedly stated, as in whole of the rest not a single new thought or idea is to be found, and I am convinced that if once the first volume is accessible in an English translation, the Govt. of India is very likely to change its opinion on this point".

"As regards the Granth of Gobind Singh, those parts of it may be translated which have any interest at all, as the FapJi and the Vichittra Natak, where he gives a sketch of his own wild life".

"His two Rahitnamas show, at any rate, how Sikhism was constituted under him, and are not very long".

Source : Progds. For-Gen., A, Aug. 1874, no. 5 (N.A.I.).

Bibliography

UNPUBLISHED SOURCES

National Archives of India, New Delhi—to be referred as N.A.I.

Proceedings, Foreign Deptt., 8th April, 1859, Numbers 141-42.

Progds. Home-Education, May 22, 1869, nos. 35-38 (N.A.I.)

Progds. For Gen., A, July 1869, nos. 68-69 (I.N.A.)

Progds. Foreign Gen., A, July 1870, nos. 67-70 (N.A.I.)

" " Nov., 1870, nos. 26-27 (N.A.I.)

" " Dec., 1870, nos. 1-2 (N.A.I.)

" " April, 1872, nos. 110-14 (N.A.I.)

" " May, 1872, nos. 6-9 (N.A.I.)

" " Feb., 1873, nos. 58-67 (N.A.I.)

" " July, 1873, nos. 34-37 (N.A.I.)

" " Sep., 1873, no. 6-10 (N.A.I.)

" " Jan., 1874, nos. 1-5 (N.A.I.)

" " A, July, 1874, nos. 1-4 (N.A.I.)

" " A, Sep., 1874, nos. 59-61 (N.A.I.)

" " A, March, 1875, nos. 38-43 (N.A.I.)

" " June, 1875, nos. 21-24 (N.A.I.)

" " January, 1877, nos. 16-17 (N.A.I.)

PUBLISHED SOURCES

Books

Ahluwalia, *M.M., Maharaja Ranjit Singh's Negotiations with the British Envoy,* C.T. Metcalfe (New Delhi, 1982).

Asoke, S.S., *Punjab Dia Lehran* (Pbi) (Patiala, 1974).

Bhadour, Attar Singh, *Sakhee Book or the Descriptions of Guru Gobind Singh's Religion and Doctrines* (Benaras, 1873).

Charles, Aitchison, *Lord Lawrence and the Reconstruction of India under the British* (Oxford, 1916).

Cust, R.N., *Linguistic and Oriental Essays* (London, 1891).

——, *Memories of Past Years of a Septuagenarian* (London, 1899).

Fauja Singh (ed.), *Historians and Historiography of the Sikhs* (New Delhi, 1978).

——, *Kuka Movement* (Motilal Banarsidass, 1965).

Ganda Singh, *Kukian de Vithia* (Pbi) (Patiala, 2000).

George Macmunn, *The History of Sikh Pioneers* (London, n.d.).

Grewal, J.S., *Historical Perspectives on Sikh Identity* (Patiala, 1997).

——, *Contesting Interpretations of Sikh Tradition* (Manohar, 1998).

Grewal, J.S. and Bal, S.S., *Guru Gobind Singh* (Chandigarh, 1987).

Griffin, L.H., *The Punjab Chiefs* (1865).

——, *The Rajas of the Punjab* (Lahore, 1870).

Gupta, Hari Ram, *History of the Sikhs,* Vol. iii (New Delhi, 1980).

Gurbachan Kaur, *Shardha Ram Philouri* (Pbi) (Patiala, 1988).

Harbans Singh, *The Heritage of the Sikhs* (Manohar, 1983).

Henery Court (ed. and tr.), *History of the Sikhs; OR, Translation of Sikhan de Raj de Vithia* (Lahore, 1888).

Jaswinder Singh, *Kuka Movement* (New Delhi, 1985).

Macauliffe, M.A., *The Sikh Religion,* 6 vols. (Satvic Books, 2000).

Mann, Gurinder Singh, *The Making of Sikh Scripture* (Oxford, 2001).

McLeod, W.H., *Early Sikh Tradition : A Study of the Janam-Sakhi* (Oxford, 1980).

——, *Exploring Sikhism* (Oxford, 2000).

McLeod, W.H., *Sikhs of the Khalsa* (Oxford, 2003).

——, *Discovering the Sikhs* (Permanent Black, 2004).

——, *Who is a Sikh* (Oxford, 1989).

Nahar Singh, *Guru Ram Singh and the Kuka Sikhs* (New Delhi, 1965).

Nayyar, G.S., *Maukhik Itihas* (Pbi) (New Delhi, 1990).

Nazer Singh, *Delhi and Punjab* (New Delhi, 1995).

Oberoi, H.S., *The Construction of Religious Boundaries* (Delhi, 1997).

Piar Singh, *Gatha Sri Adi Granth and the Controversy* (Michigan, 1996).

Pritam Singh, *Sikhan de Raj de Vithia* (Pbi) (Jallundhar, 1956).

Report on the Punjab Missionary Conference held at Lahore in Dec.-January 1862-63 (Lodiana, the American Presbyterian Mission Press, n.d.).

Surjit Hans, *A Reconstruction of Sikh History From Sikh Literature* (Jallundhar, 1988).

Sagar, S.S., *Hukamnamas of Guru Teg Bahadur* (Amritsar, 2002).

Sethi, R.R., *The Mighty and Shrewd Maharaja* (Delhi, 1960).

Suri, Sohan Lal, *Umdat Tawarikhi Daftar,* II and III.

Trumpp, Ernest, *The Adi Granth* (Motilal Banarsidass, 1997).

Articles

Cust, R.N., 'Guru Nanak the Indian Reformer', *The Panjab Past and Present,* Vol. iii, 1969, pp. 158-68.

Nazer Singh, 'The Khalsa Towards the Singh Sabha', in, *Proceedings Punjab History Conference,* 1999.

——, 'Khalsa and its Modern Historians', *Journal of Sikh Studies,* Vol. xviii, no.1, 1999.

Surjit Hans, 'The Secular Heritage of the Sikhs', in *Sikh History and Religion in the Twentieth Century* (ed.) by Joseph T.O.' Connel and others (Manohar, 1990).

——, 'Early Sikh Tradition', in, *Journal of Regional History,* Vol. i, 1980, pp. 175-88.

Index

I